AF477763

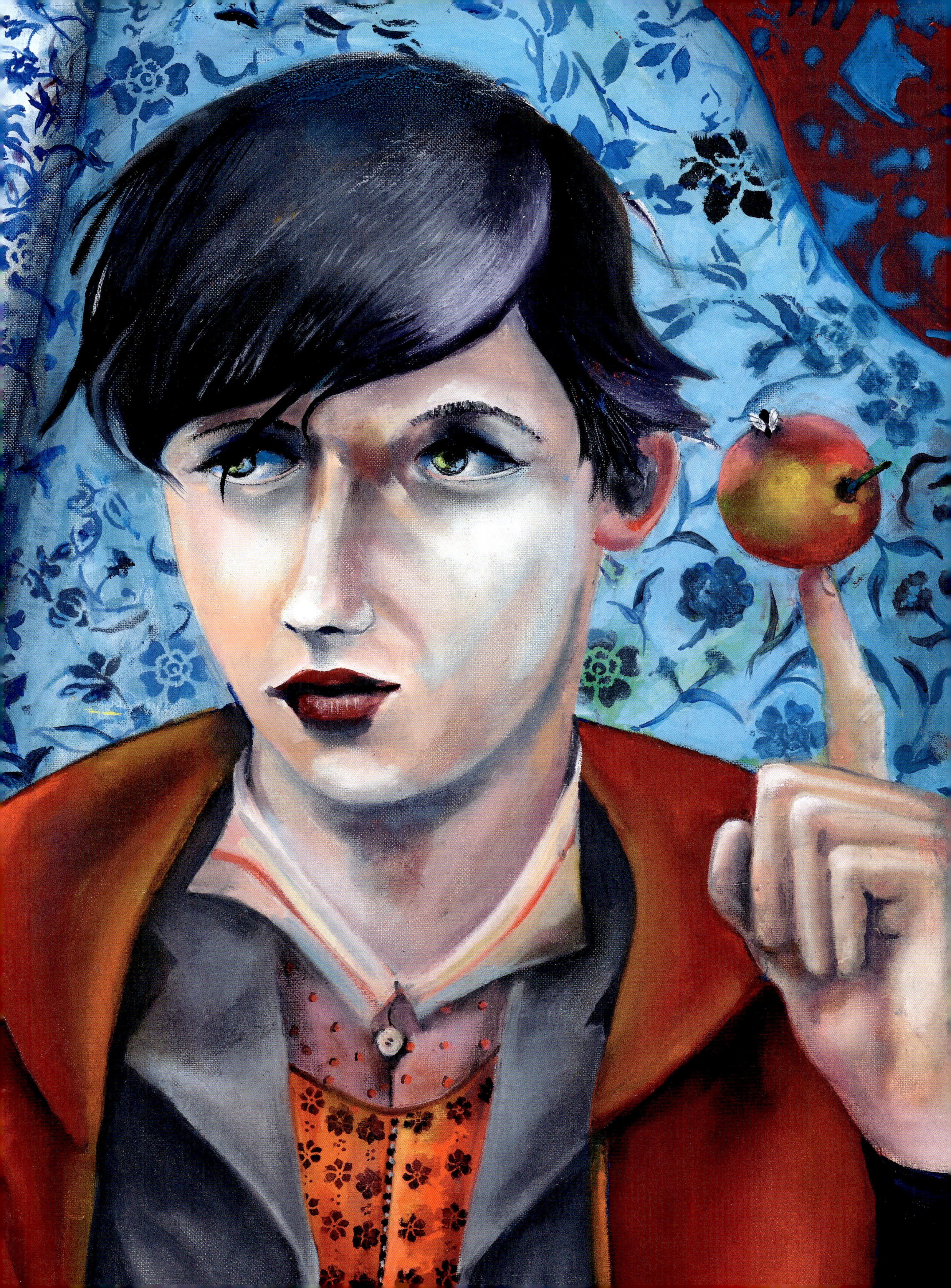

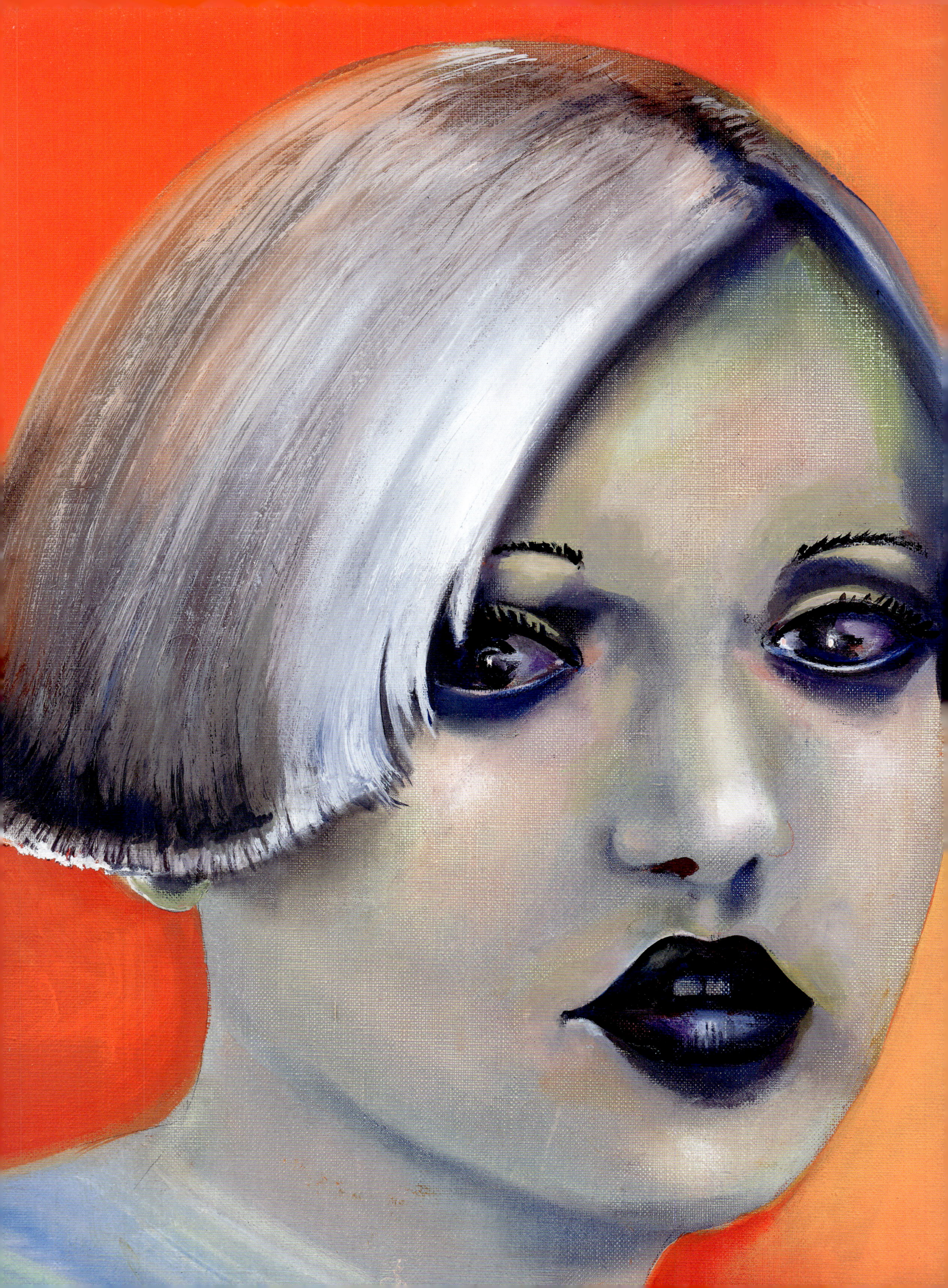

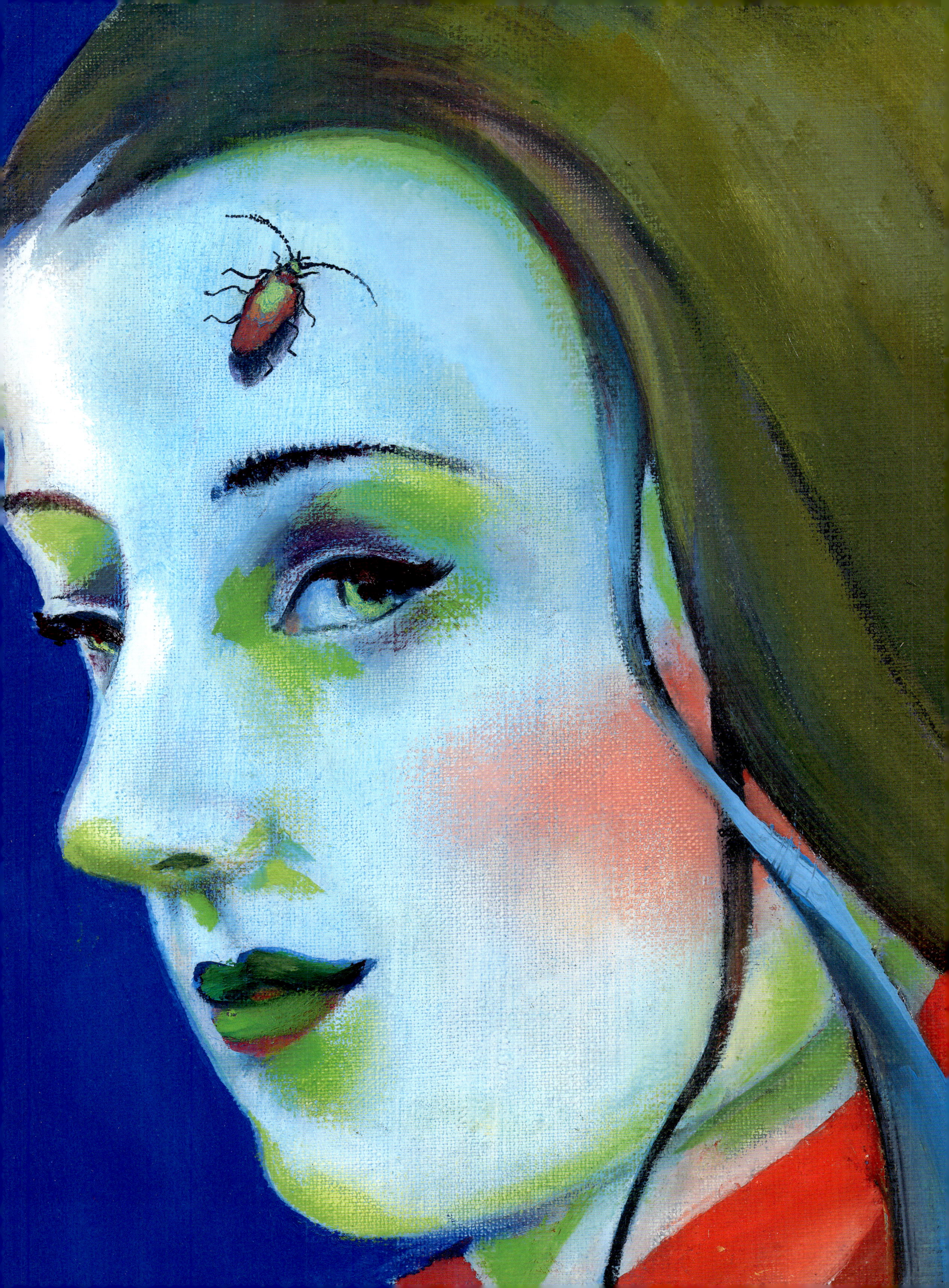

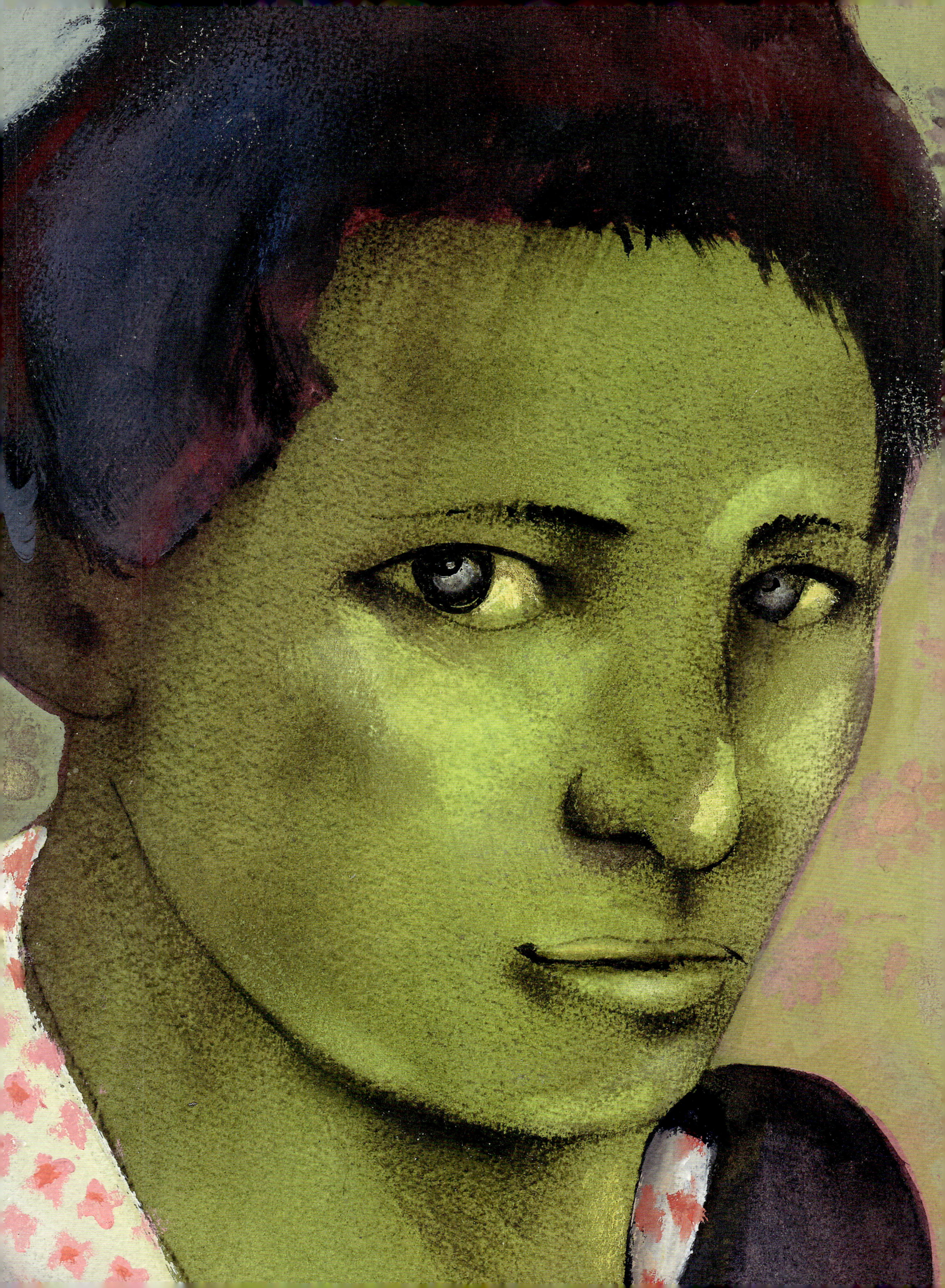

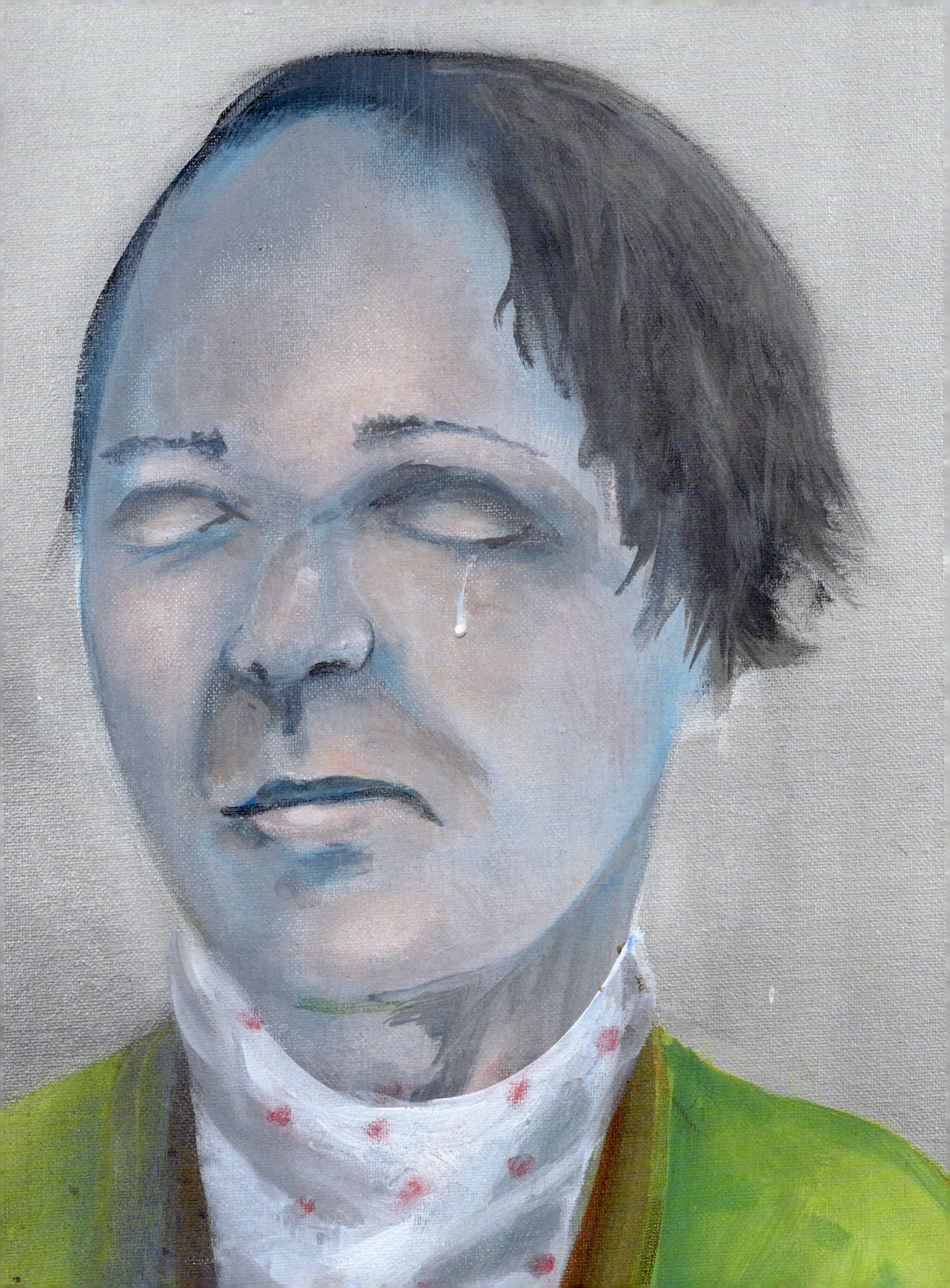

ĹG

LÉVY GORVY

MARTIAL RAYSSE

VISAGES

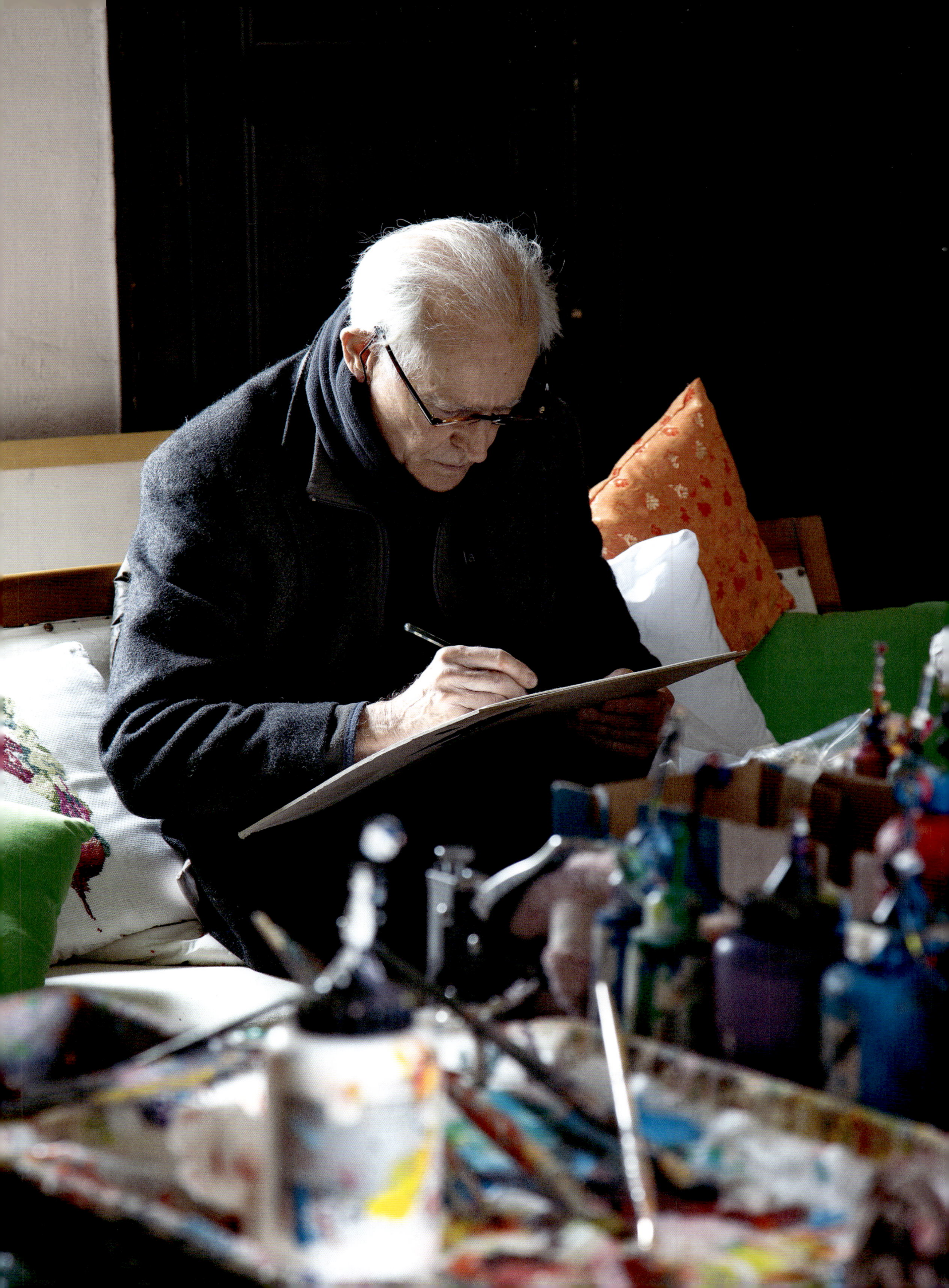

Contents

Acknowledgments

Expression, or the face, overflows images.

—EMMANUEL LEVINAS

What do we see when we see a face?

A stranger gazes out from under curled lashes, a secret on their lips, their skin alight with green envy, or pallor, or the neon glow of city lights. An insect crawls atop their forehead or the canvas' surface, lit in the same unreal tones.

Another *visage* has a faraway look, eyes cast to the side in regret, or contemplation, or resignation. The sea swells behind, about to overtake their solitude.

Martial Raysse's faces implore without speaking, relate without touching, demand without asking. Raysse first began painting figuratively in 1961, and since then has remained boldly committed to depicting the human *visage*—in all its forthrightness, its enigmas and vagaries, its tendencies to express and then hide, its attempts at masquerade.

Despite its singularity, the face can be hauntingly vague, even anonymous: faces peer at us from billboards and behind screens, tempting our desires to possess or replicate; *visages* without names or histories emerge from uncaptioned photographs and portraits. With irony, daring, and exuberance, Raysse works within these complexities, never simplifying, never satisfied with the easy answer. His faces are sometimes brightly colored, dazzling us; other times reduced to symbols and grids; elsewhere depicting recognizable celebrities or mythical archetypes. The brooding loner, gazing outward with penetrating eyes; the flirt, peering out from heavy eyelids; the mischievous drunkard; the clown; the goddess—all find themselves under Raysse's brush, their beauty and artifice intertwined to create images rife with mystery.

Raysse's visages are traversed by social and cultural signs, laden with expression and pathos, styled and presented just so: we feel we can almost touch the artist's subjects, hear their voices, *know* them. A small flower blossom is held in a lipsticked mouth; a worm-eaten apple balances on a pointed finger; blind eyes cry mournful tears; dark lips part to speak…Raysse's *visages* tempt us with their ambiguities. The artist works in the pauses between words, the gaps between representation and reality.

Ten years after first taking brush to canvas, Raysse placed himself within this very pause: he retreated from the art world for ten years to question his own work deeply, to demand of his *visages* both relevance and truth. This pursuit led him chasing after timeless archetypes, conversing with Baroque masters and contemporary advertisements alike, crossing Minimalism, Conceptual art, politics, and history, returning again to the face in all its possibility. Through questioning and criticism, Raysse has remained faithful to figuration. His work is consistently surprising, challenging, lyrical.

In surveying the full range of his portraits, it became clear to us that Raysse is as much a master anthropologist of his own place and time as he is an artist. He deeply understands the fabric of society, and expresses what he sees in allegory, fable, and myth. Continually searching, he demands a more exuberant form, a more brilliant truth. This deliberation is transformed into immediacy on canvas: in figuration, Raysse does not hesitate or compromise, and, with incredible daringness, pushes always toward an art that more accurately captures life.

This exhibition and publication would not have been possible without the support and enthusiasm of so many:

First and foremost, our deep gratitude to the artist, Martial Raysse. Martial, thank you for your trust. Over the course of nearly two decades of friendship, it has been a privilege to watch your approach to figuration grow, become increasingly refined, be challenged, and to see you always come home again to representation. We are honored by our new collaboration, and thank you for allowing us to commemorate your *visages* with this exhibition.

A profound thank you to Caroline Bourgeois. Caroline, we are indebted to your thoroughness, your commitment, and your willingness to share your scholarship. Your work at the Pinault Collection is an inspiration, and our conversations are treasured sources of knowledge and insight.

Our gratitude to Jane Livingston, whose thorough and necessary essay elegantly describes the link between poetry and painting in Raysse's practice.

A special thanks to Leopoldine Core, whose luminous poem, "The Bird," does in language what Raysse's *visages* do in paint, and speaks to the continued relevance of an artist who so earnestly engages questions of femininity, beauty, and artifice.

Sincere gratitude is due to Clara Touboul, director of exhibitions at the gallery, whose perseverance and ingenuity touched all aspects of this project. Clara, your unwavering dedication to our exhibitions and publications is an invaluable force at the gallery, and this book and exhibition would not have been possible without your leadership.

A proud thank-you to the team at the gallery who embraced this project and made it possible, especially Amelia Brown, for her coordination of this publication, and Courtney Fiske and Katie Langjahr for their research.

To Mark Nelson and Meg Becker at McCall Associates, Susan Delson, and Massimo Tonolli, thank you for your steadfast commitment to our publications.

DOMINIQUE LÉVY

BRETT GORVY

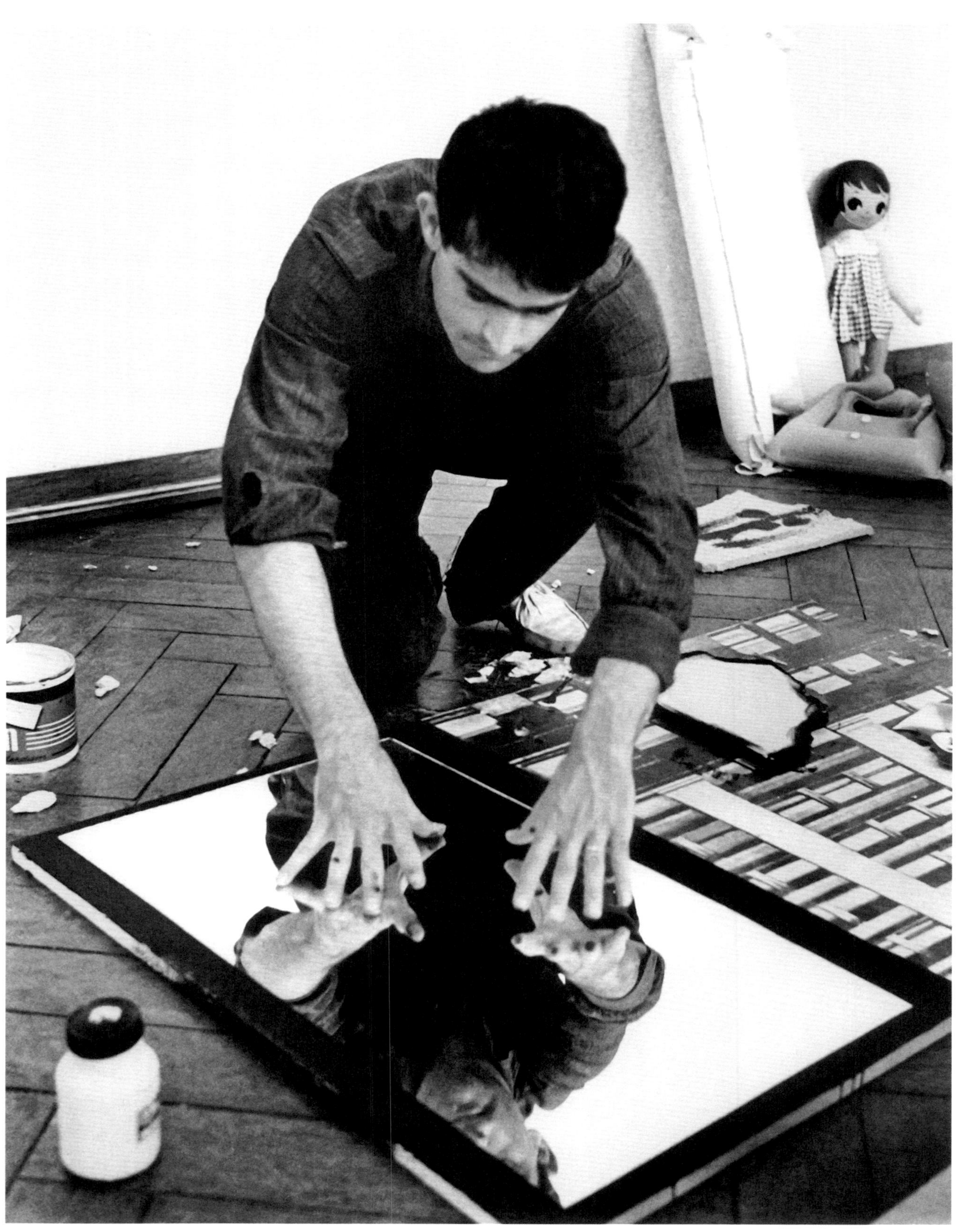

Raysse during the installation of *Dynamisch Labyrinth* (known as *Dylaby*), Stedelijk Museum, Amsterdam, 1962

Martial Raysse: Je suis un poète

JANE LIVINGSTON

The paintings of Martial Raysse shown in this time and place, New York in early 2018, will come as a surprise to many who encounter them. From the perspective of fifty years of hindsight, it might seem impossible that a brilliant and accomplished European artist of one's own generation, lionized in his native France, should be so little known in the United States—all the more because he was very much a part of the international scene in the 1960s. Raysse lived in both New York and Los Angeles in that decade, and consorted with many of the important American artists of the moment. But after returning to France for good in the early 1970s, he virtually disappeared from both America's precincts and its art-world conversation.

It is difficult now to convey the pugilistic intensity of the politics both of art criticism and art making during the 1960s and 1970s. From the perspective of an American museum curator and critic of contemporary art, new developments in New York, Los Angeles, San Francisco, London, and Paris came accompanied by a frantic *positioning* of style and ideology. An artist had to fit into an "ism"—Abstract Expressionism or Conceptualism or Minimalism, Op art or Pop art or Arte Povera, *tachisme* or Nouveau Réalisme. The pressure on the curatorial and art critics' communities was exceeded only by that on the artists who seemed, often despite themselves, compelled to stake out a territory. Given the (often inadvertently) doctrinaire quality of the era, it is a kind of miracle that so much sentient, fresh, and enduring work emerged from its hothouse environment; indeed, we prize this chapter in twentieth-century art history nearly as highly as the legendary moment that emerged before and during the First World War, when Matisse and Braque and so many others ascended to their incredible heights. But of course, legions of promising artists of that era have vanished from history. Martial Raysse is not one of them.

The period following World War II occasioned a difficult pivot for visual artists in Europe. France had kept the fire of cultural vanguardism at a roaring pitch for at least fifty years leading up to this second disastrous war, but by the 1950s its appetite for aesthetic competitiveness was at a low ebb. But if sheer inventive energy seemed to wane, the artists of France remained hyper-alert to what was happening across the Atlantic, in New York, where so many European artists had emigrated in the 1930s and 1940s. A few, like Martial Raysse, looked to both New York and Los Angeles for invigoration. He found much in both places to fuel his early experiments. But, having survived the war on its own turf, these European artists were generally more *politically* informed and motivated than their American counterparts. For them, it wasn't so easy to adopt either the language of the extreme abstracting of pure form or that of the new mass culture. For a deeply rooted Frenchman like Raysse, it would prove not enough to simply embrace The New. Now, fifty years later, we can see more clearly what this division—between the American optimism and energy, and the French and Italian artists' war-exhaustion and anxiety—meant for the art they made, and continue to make.

As a curator at the Los Angeles County Museum of Art, I was living and working in that city in the late 1960s. In my capacity as monthly reviewer for *Artforum* magazine, I wrote about the exhibition of Martial Raysse's new work in 1967 at Virginia Dwan's gallery. Its sensibility struck me as surpassingly odd, and I remember being baffled, challenged, and intrigued. It was not easy to assign an "ism" to it, although its most obvious attribute was a referencing of other art. My first impression was of an artist fascinated by Pop art but almost risibly, self-consciously "French" in its adoption. Its signature image was the wonderful painting of Jean-August-Dominique Ingres's redoubtable *Grande*

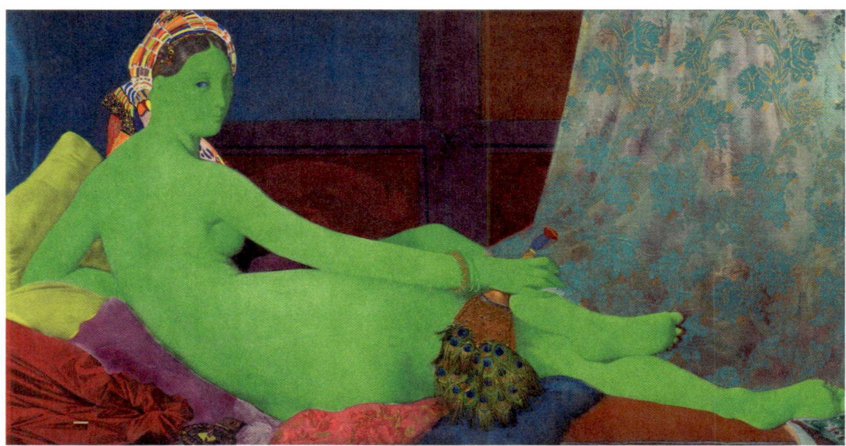

1. *Made in Japan*, 1964. Photomechanical reproductions and wallpaper with airbrush ink, gouache, ink, tacks, peacock feathers, and plastic flies on paper mounted on fiberboard, 51 ⅛ × 96 ¼ inches (129.8 × 244.3 cm). Collection of the Hirshhorn Museum and Sculpture Garden. Gift of Joseph H. Hirshhorn, 1972

Odalisque, transformed by Raysse into a reptilian-green, languidly mocking, full-length reclining nude artifact (fig. 1). The peacock feathers in the fan she held were real, appended to the surface. This classic figure in the exalted history of French painting, with her famous three-quarter-turned face, now sported a cloth turban translated into a jauntily colorful, African-inspired textile. It was a telling detail in the artist's reconfiguring, and to this arresting act of intellectual property theft lent its character of both redeeming humor and strangely loving respect. The transmogrified image wasn't so much cynically appropriated as affectionately transported into the 1960s realm of licentious facsimile. What I now believe I missed about this exhibition was its pungent undertone of dissatisfaction. I was too young, or the war and its depredations too distant, to allow me to see the bitterness and intensity that underlaid the artist's vulgarization of his own precious legacy. What I didn't miss, and what has endured to this day, was its character of intractable idiosyncrasy.

That exhibition in Los Angeles also included a work that incorporated elements made of plastic tubing and bottles filled with red fluid, as well as a sculpture of a flower pot. These reflected, in part, Raysse's temporary affinity to the French assemblagist Arman, who was enjoying somewhat more exposure in the American art scene of the time—as was Yves Klein, another artist who belonged, under the rubric of Nouveau Réalisme, to the coterie to which Raysse belonged in his early years. (Raysse, Arman, and Klein were all originally from Provence, and were known as "les Niçois.") This term "Nouveau Réalisme" was introduced by the French critic Pierre Restany; its members actually signed a text he formulated in 1960 as a statement of intent. The artists who worked and showed under its rubric shared a desire to eschew "pure art," espousing an art that both incorporated and lived ordinary daily reality and its contemporary appurtenances. It would be a rather short-lived phenomenon whose name didn't very well describe what it embodied, which wasn't any kind of "realism" at all. Its members also included Jean Tinguely—who, like Klein, is associated with the literal physical destruction or self-destruction of objects, and/or performance art—and the Conceptualist Daniel Spoerri. Niki de Saint Phalle, whose environmentally scaled works are aggressively whimsical and theatrical, became associated with the group and became relatively well known in America.

Because of Raysse's age (he was born in 1936), his nationality, and his interest in undermining the preciousness and artificiality of "high aesthetics," it was natural for him to be subsumed under the Nouveau Réalisme rubric. But he was probably never deeply committed to this association, even at its most self-proclaiming moment in 1960. By the 1970s Raysse became radically disenchanted with whatever allegiance to its precepts he might once have held. After living in New York for a year, followed by five years (1963–68) in Los Angeles, he returned to France to participate in the revolutionary Paris eruption of May 1968. Given his deep commitment to the bold intellectual and political leftist movement of his time (both parents had been valorous members of the French Resistance under German/French–collaborationist occupation), he naturally had to be present in Paris when its ideals seemed to be bearing tangible fruit. It was a heady moment, and for Raysse it would occasion a permanent return to France.

Nobody, of course, could have known that any true structural changes in the social fabric, so earnestly awaited in those months of contagious hope, would soon be swept away by in the inexorable capitalist forces of the military/industrial/consumerist networks that engulfed the Western world and its governments in the last third of the twentieth century.

Some of the commentary on Raysse's early work aligns it with a cultural obsession noticed by Roland Barthes: a certain atmosphere of "health, super-sanitation" that permeated France in the postwar years. More than once, the concept of a "clean woman" is evoked, and Raysse himself, in a statement published in the Virginia Dwan exhibition brochure in 1967, says: "I wanted my works to possess the serene self-evidence of mass-produced refrigerators...to have the look of new, sterile, inalterable visual hygiene." This idea is borne out in one of the devices used by both Raysse and Arman in the 1960s: the vitrine or Plexiglas box, containing collected objects whose significance resided in their choosing, rather than their making, by the artist. For Raysse, this moment in his work would prove less indicative of an interest in the Dada-based idea of the found object than of a deep engagement with three-dimensional objects, which he would periodically return to, couched in the language of familiar sculptural craftsmanship. (He has worked in many sculptural media, from cast bronze to papier-mâché.) His early, photo-derived images would essentially be displaced by a commitment to old-fashioned draftsmanship, and an abiding respect for the traditions of European painting in particular. Though his art would never lose its early atmosphere of quirkiness, its primary reference would come to be nothing more nor less than European art history itself.

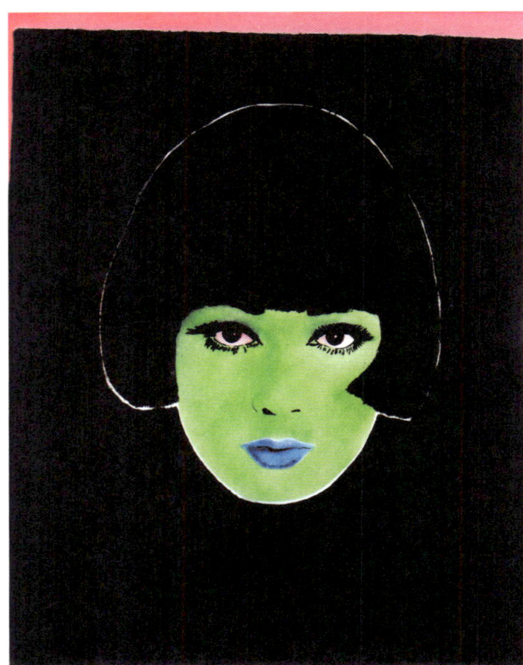

2. *Belle des nuages*, 1965. Flock and fluorescent paint on canvas, 58 ⅞ × 46 $^{7}/_{16}$ × 2 $^{3}/_{16}$ inches (149.5 × 118 × 5.5 cm). Pinault Collection

One of the pervasive issues in the artistic conversation of the 1960s was photography. Though Walter Benjamin's writings on "mechanical reproduction" wouldn't be widely taken up until a little later (via Roland Barthes and Susan Sontag), the importance of the medium did not escape Raysse. During his years in Los Angeles he was fascinated by Xerox technology; the way he used color refers blatantly to the quality of advertising reproductions of the era, and he wasn't afraid to use the tricks of the trade. He was also a filmmaker, and used both still photography and moving imagery in his cinematic works. But all of this, according to the artist now, became less and less relevant to him—in his own words, he decided he "didn't want to be the French Pop artist."[1] One sub-genre of his early Pop-influenced art, however, established a format that he never abandoned: namely, the series of heads, or faces, of beautiful women, undisguisedly borrowed from Andy Warhol's serigraphed faces, of which Marilyn Monroe's is perhaps the archetype. Raysse borrowed directly from this idea in a number of striking, sometimes neon-hued faces of beautiful women, both famous and anonymous, in works from the 1960s that directly prefigure works in the present exhibition (fig. 2).

What might have appeared as an undertone of dismissiveness of the artistic concerns of the 1960s and 1970s now appears to be something different. While Raysse both embraced the techniques of photography and mistrusted them, and while he made a point of turning his back on an association with Nouveau Réalisme or any other group, he always embraced the ordinary arts of representation. What he fundamentally did not like and did not practice was the numerous forms of "abstract" or "non-objective" art. His wrestling with this idea—as a man of conscience, self-awareness, and a fiercely strong-minded aesthetic disposition—plays into many of his artistic decisions. Raysse experimented with several interesting threads of his immediate predecessors and contemporaries, rejected what came to bore him, and embarked on a journey of making sculptures and paintings that belong to a long tradition. That tradition, of course, includes slightly outré figures like Salvador Dalí and Giorgio de Chirico, two artists he knew and admired. Both drew equally upon the realms of classicism and Surrealism, and, using a highly literary formal language, found ways to create something unique and enduring. It is significant and poignant to note that Raysse characterizes both of these artists as having become "disillusioned. After their early great periods, their art collapsed."

Raysse fully participated in the cultural life of his time, and would have been well aware of both the artistic and philosophical ideas that infused the European and American/Latin American climate of his generation. But the key to the artist's concerns, visible now in retrospect, is the fact that his work would gradually be consumed by his "return" to the customary media and formats of drawing, painting, and sculpture. Around the time he turned forty, he took a long look at what he wanted to do, and decided that he was simply an artist who belonged firmly within the tradition inherited by his cultural birthright. His antecedents and touchstones were housed in the museums of Europe. This does not imply, however, that he was temperamentally drawn to any form of academicism; he is a fundamentally independent spirit whose iconoclasm is always in tension with his aesthetic conservatism. And the fact that his work always has something of the flavor of the "outsider," or "visionary" or "self-taught" artist is because, in fact, he is a self-taught painter and sculptor. One salient difference is in the materials he uses to paint: though he often employs traditional distemper and occasionally oil, on canvas or panel, he has become unusually proficient in the medium of synthetic polymer (acrylic) paint. Among his peers, Raysse has become one of the most dedicated and skilled proponents of the acrylic medium.

The facts of Raysse's biographical trajectory of course figure heavily in his later development. He was born in Golfe-Juan, Vallauris, to a family of potters. His earliest years were inevitably fraught with contradiction: on one hand, he was brought up in an idyllic geographic and cultural environment—beautiful seaside landscapes, bucolic provincial rituals, seat of some of the greatest art of the early twentieth century. On the other hand, by the time he was a young child, war and the nightmare of German occupation descended upon him and his family. When he was eight, he was wrenched from his bed by a German soldier, an event he says marked him permanently. The combination, in his youth, of the example of his parents' tenacious resistance to the pull of accommodation; his existence in a relatively isolated and non-cosmopolitan world that, even in the depths of wartime, preserved its umbilical cord to the great metropolis; and the imperatives of his own nature, that of a poet, a non-conforming spirit who always hungered to experience and understand the mysteries of his world—all these things would define his later artistic journey. He studied literature at the university in Nice while also attending classes at François Bret's School of Decorative Arts. Later, refusing conscription into the Algerian War, he was briefly committed to a

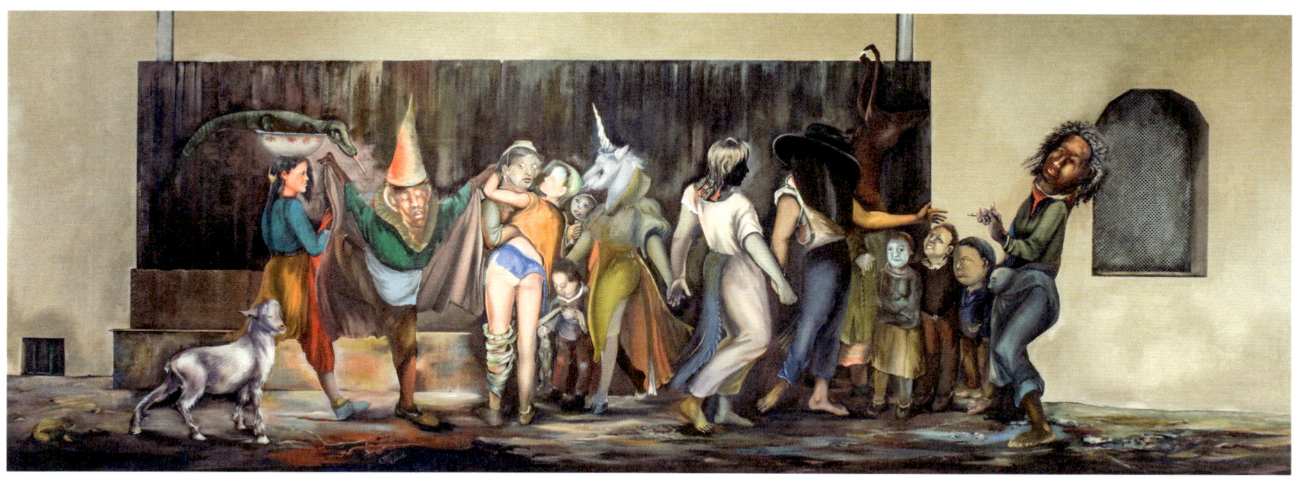

3. *Le Carnaval à Périgueux*, 1992. Distemper on canvas, 118 ⅛ × 315 15/16 inches (300 × 800 cm). Pinault Collection

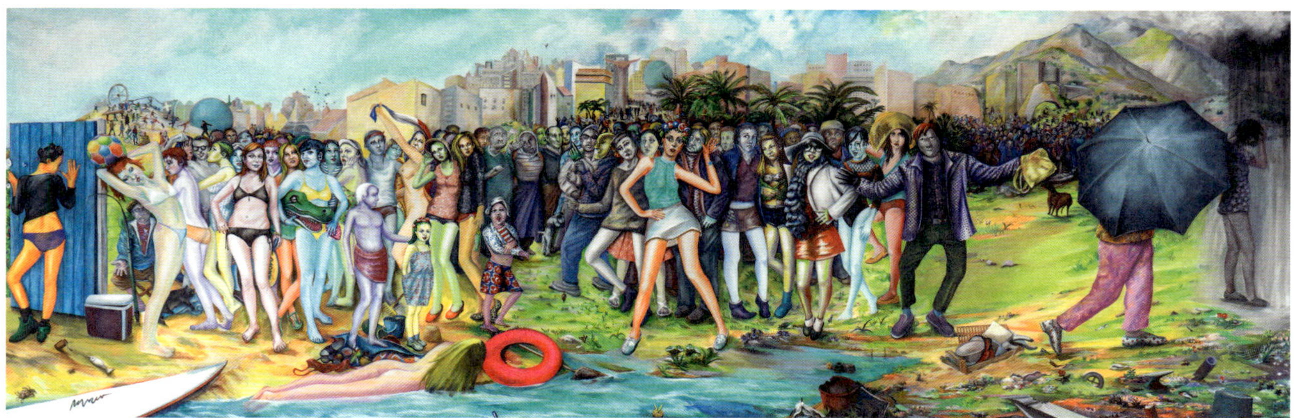

4. *Ici Plage, comme ici-bas*, 2012. Oil and acrylic binder on canvas, 118 ⅛ × 354 5/16 inches (300 × 900 cm). Pinault Collection

psychiatric hospital in Marseille, after which, in 1960, he moved to Paris. By the time he left France to live in New York and Los Angeles he had imbibed some of the atmosphere of France's rich intellectual/cultural heritage, even while refusing to entirely buy into its various philosophical seductions. His independence, and a stubborn attachment to his own way of interpreting what he experienced, were well established by the time he was in his thirties.

Gradually, as he settled into a long and productive working life—based in the self-renovated farm structures in rural Dordogne that he bought in 1972—the artist has produced an ambitious body of paintings, sculptures, and assemblages. Every few years an enormous, mural-scaled piece has emerged, beginning with the stage-set-like *Raysse Beach* in 1962 and including the huge paintings *Le Carnaval* à *Périgueux* (1992; fig. 3) and *Ici Plage, comme ici-bas* (2012; fig. 4). As Raysse's vocabulary developed into elaborate, wall-sized group compositions, incorporating dozens of figures and complex skeins of symbolic objects and referents, one stylistic element remained from his earliest days: the use of a peculiar, sometimes intentionally noxious palette. As a young innovator absorbing the ethos of American art in the 1960s, Raysse was fascinated by neon light. The palette in his heroically scaled paintings incorporates electric pinks, greens, blues, and oranges that derive directly from the quality of neon light first glimpsed, he says, in childhood, in a blue advertising sign in downtown Nice. He has incorporated actual neon, attached to canvases or comprising freestanding objects, from the 1960s to recent years.

Raysse's aesthetic and conceptual preoccupations are expressed in the same way that poets, over the arcs of their careers, visit and revisit certain themes. It is as though a reservoir of personae or events is deeply embedded in his unconscious life and continuously plumbed for its contents. One of his primal vocabularies derives (if not literally, imaginatively) from the prehistoric cave art that surrounded his birth place and his chosen adult home near Bergerac. In his self-identification as "a poet first and foremost," he titles nearly all of his works, often in ways that are transparent only to himself. (Some of the poets he mentions as especially important to him are Dante, Yeats, Leopardi, Mallarmé, Rimbaud and Nerval.) He insists that, like a poem, each of his works should be entirely self-contained in its unique spirit, each fully present in itself. This is what he strives for above all; what he dislikes, above all, is "teaching (or learning) about art as a logical lineage." The term he uses to describe what he has rebelled against all his life is "rhetoric." He doesn't want rhetorical criticism or thought to apply to his work from within or without—although he reserves the right to criticize the rhetoricians. As an example of the mistakes that have been made by the art-historical rhetoric of recent times, he says, "The Impressionists weren't revolting against representational art. They were revolting against the bad art of the salon painters."

Raysse's art is centered in poetic imagery, and even the most concrete and ordinary objects and beings are rendered poetic in his hands. Perhaps the most important image or theme of his oeuvre is that of the woman. It is a subject that appears in widely varied forms, in virtually every phase of his work. The female figure was central to the oeuvre when he was still engaged with ideas about photo-reproduction and has continued, even more saliently, in the much longer period during which the artist has turned himself into a painter and sculptor in the art-historical tradition. Raysse made his first head of a woman in 1961. One cannot avoid comparing his female heads, in their earliest manifestation, with Andy Warhol's portraits of Monroe, Elizabeth Taylor, et al., rendered in chromatically variegated series, flat and often neon-hued, reductively composed, and reproduced serigraphically. Raysse, like Warhol, represented iconic, beautiful women in this mode, including Brigitte Bardot but more often less famous or anonymous figures. His female heads of the 1960s, such as *Ta mouche Pauline* (1966; fig. 5), use photography directly; this one, with its appended plastic fly, presages his use of insects in later paintings of female heads. Simultaneously, in the 1960s, the artist made a number of works that expropriated famous art-historical females, such as Tintoretto's nude *Susanna* (fig. 6) and Cranach's nude *Diana* (fig. 7), though none of these was used in as many permutations as Ingres's *Odalisaque* (fig. 1). But, as we see in the present exhibition, any generalized or satiric way of treating the female head or figure would not become the artist's truest incarnation of this essential subject. Instead, what has emerged in the artist's heads (and sometimes torsos)—primarily female but sometimes male or androgyne—is a singular group of pictures that cannot be equated with those of any other artist. Raysse's small paintings of faces and heads are interrelated but not serial, each combining an atmosphere of quirkiness and individuality, each with its own strange character of self-contained emotional connotation. These pictures may be said to distill both Raysse's skillful technique and his extremely literary aesthetic attitude. Both his

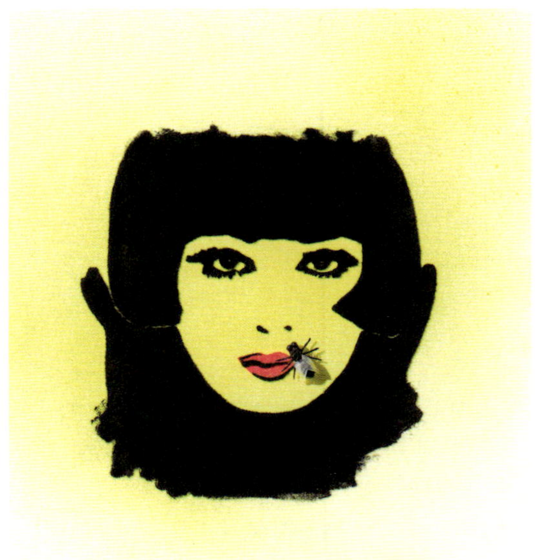

5. *Ta mouche Pauline*, 1966. Mixed media and plastic fly glued to glass, 11 7/16 × 10 5/8 inches (29 × 27 cm). Collection Martial Raysse

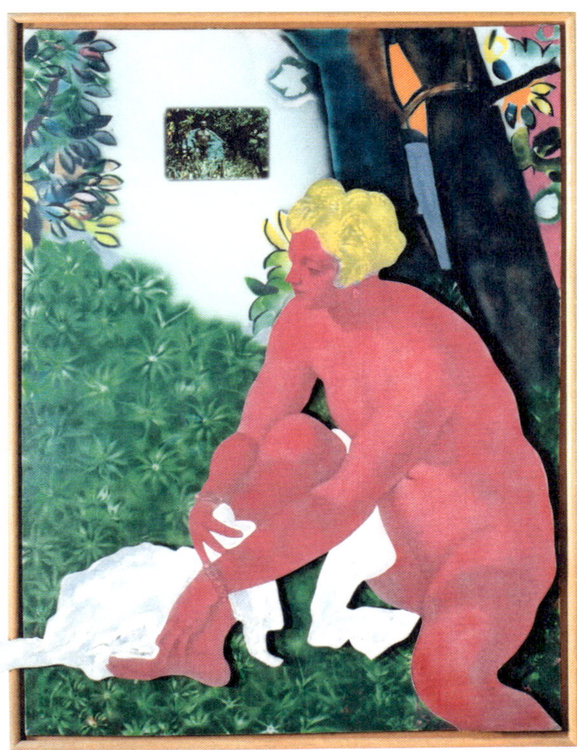

6. *Suzanna, Suzanna*, 1964. Collage, oil on canvas, and projection of film *Arman dans le role du vieillard*, 75 9⁄16 × 55 9⁄16 × 3 15⁄16 inches (192 × 141 × 10 cm). Private collection

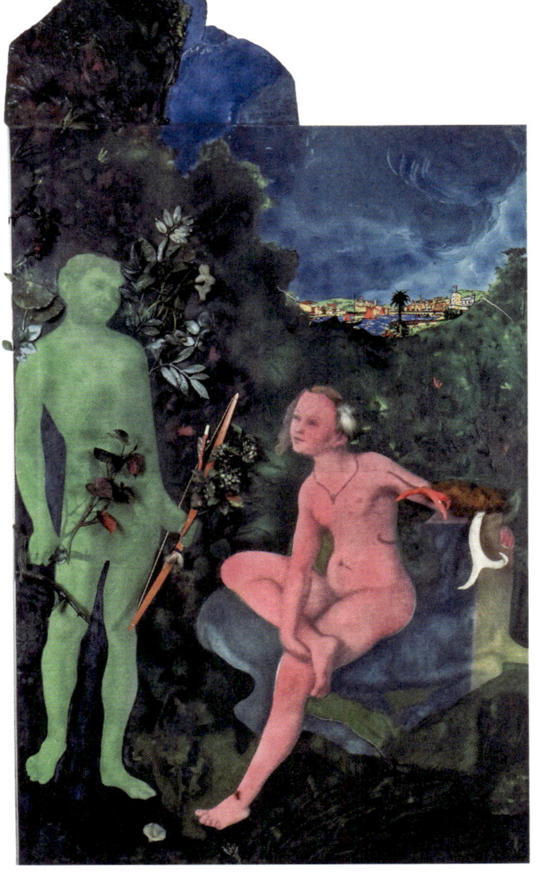

7. *Conversation printanière*, 1964. Oil, collage, and assemblage of various materials on canvas wooden panel, 89 15⁄16 × 50 inches (228.5 × 127 cm). Pinault Collection

technique and his poetic sensibility are notably diffuse and often difficult to parse, especially in the more famous panoramic or multi-part works he has made over the years—but also in his most seemingly reductive heads. They are not exactly traditional portraits, though their models are eminently real, nor are they studies of the human physiognomy. They are at once metaphorical and particular, poetic and literal.

Two small paintings in this exhibition, *Ô Léa !* (page 75) and *Songeuse Roxane* (page 63), both of 2013, illustrate this recurring modality in Raysse's oeuvre of the small-format female head. The artist restricts both the size and shape—these works are about sixteen inches and twenty-five inches square, respectively. Each poses a woman's head against a relatively neutral, monochromatic background. Both subjects are, at first glance, generically attractive young women whose demeanors are smoothly made-up, psychologically protected. The strangeness and power in each of these apparently straightforward images reveals itself only on further investigation. *Ô Léa !* is cross-eyed, and upon her nose sits an insect—a three-dimensional object attached to the canvas. Suddenly the picture becomes a sort of joke, a cartoon-like visual anecdote. This revelation is disconcerting in the extreme, not because it is a playful little bijoux, but because it is not. *Ô Léa !* has a sharp impact. She holds the wall, cannot be ignored, and her slight edginess is produced not only by the crossed eyes but by the entire shape of her outlined head and neck and slightly distorted shoulder line. Her silhouette, indeed, powerfully supersedes the narrative event of the crossed eyes and the insect they converge on. And we don't quite know why this is so.

Songeuse Roxane projects a similarly charged aura of existing, inexplicably, on multiple levels. Here, a characteristically disconcerting palette combines with a powerful silhouette and a sensuously featured subject to create something that grows and changes with prolonged scrutiny.

And again, we don't quite know why. At first it is the slightly bilious colors—grayish-greenish skin, glowing orange ground—that appear to create the disquieting tone. Yet her fashionably bobbed hair, the dark, shiny cupid's-bow lips, the meticulously lined and shadowed eye makeup, lend to Roxane a quality of safeguarded equanimity. Even in her fully formed self-possession, she remains vulnerable in the artificiality of her presentation. Her theatricality is held in perfect stillness. On close examination, we see that the application of acrylic paint on her face is very thin; the weave of the canvas shows through palpably. She is the opposite of heavily made-up. To discover this odd detail—most of these works seem at first so opaquely executed, with their peculiar, ambiguous colors and their old-fashioned modeling—is to grasp how subtle and skilled is the artist's command of his acrylic medium. Other faces in Raysse's paintings are similarly treated, with pigment so thinly applied that the texture of the underlying cloth is exposed—while adjacent passages, especially those of bare limbs, are richly modeled with multihued pigment. Often flesh is more fleshly in the arms and legs than in the complex visages.

In his obsessively rendered depictions of women, Raysse consciously emphasizes the overall outlines of their bodies. He views the outer silhouette of hair, face, neck, and shoulders in each work as an element that, in itself, should communicate a defining emotional tenor. This aspect of any work is so fundamentally important to the artist that if it isn't there, and if it isn't distinctive only to itself, the painting doesn't work. Related to this imperative, perhaps, is the importance of titles. Raysse says he has a "horror of *sans titre*," and that he usually selects a title while the work is in progress or later. He is also capable of attaching different titles to startlingly similar works, as we see with *Ô Léa !*, which has a closely related version called *Comment ça va Irma ?* (2013; fig. 8). Many such instances exist, in which the same or similar devices, which clearly have their own iconographic significance for the artist—the bug on the nose, a butterfly placed on a face near the lips—figure repeatedly in works made over a span of many decades. These many reiterated elements, sometimes obvious and sometimes hidden, create a running poetic subtext or code that undergirds nearly every aspect of Raysse's visual language.

A work whose very compositional heart can be found in its elegant figurative silhouette is *Mais oui PULCHRA !* (2016; page 57). This extraordinary painting measures approximately 63 × 44 inches, with its upright composition divided into elongated thirds by a centered figure flanked by flat areas of monochrome green on either side. Its psychological center is established by the image of a seated woman shown from the back, wearing only transparent lace panties. Her sinuous form essentializes Raysse's use of the rhythmic female outline to establish a mood; her flesh is rendered with characteristic, porcelain-like opulence. Since she is seated, facing away from the viewer, her legs are absent from the picture. Her lower body, with its burgundy-colored lingerie and a clumsily "decorative" swag of drapery at her left, is counterpoised by a small still-life passage on the lower right—which, on scrutiny, emerges as a humorous, slightly kitschy comment on the still-life genre itself. All of this, including the inclusion of at least one element that resides outside the logical parameters of the scene, is familiar in the artist's realm of imaging. What lifts this composition out of the expected in Raysse's world is the top part of the canvas, where the artist has left the work "unfinished." The outline of the woman's head is sketched in with charcoal, as though to map the contours of the finished figure to come. The swiftly executed charcoal lines appear upon an interrupted rectangular ground that suggests a canvas-within-a-canvas. The flesh-colored paint that describes her long, elegant back and the top of her right arm morphs, at the top, into a nebulous, translucent smear of paint drifting into unaccounted territory. We feel that we are experiencing the artist's own insight, as he grasps that to place a fully formed head on this gorgeously limned body would be, at best, a gratuitous act—and at worst a violation of the spirit of the piece. The "unfinished" energy of the work, which cannot be described or explained, becomes everything.

It seems evident that Martial Raysse's exploration of complex implied narrative in some of his recent paintings has become more inner-directed and contemplative, less referential to other art and literature. His many allusions to Greek myth and Christian iconography increasingly give way to small dramas of his own poetic invention. Such a work is *QUE VEUX TU DIRE MON BEL AMI* of 2017 (page 41), whose protagonist's sexual identity seems ambiguous. Here an adolescent boy—or is it a boyish young woman?—is depicted from the waist up, holding a piece of paper (a letter?) in the right hand and balancing an apple on the index finger of the left. "What do you want to say, my friend? What are you trying to say?" Is it not appropriate to ask this of the artist when pondering this painting? A sort of lightheartedness resides in this question, and in the picture's decorative conceit: an uncurling scroll of flowered fabric (or wallpaper?), set behind the figure to remind of us of its own cunning artifice and inscrutability.

If *QUE VEUX TU DIRE MON BEL AMI* is intentionally playful and ambiguous, *NOW* (2017; page 67), is quite the reverse. This work, the largest in the present exhibition, illustrates the idea that while our world is in crisis, some of us can and do go blithely about our own business. We continue in our narcissistic, selfishly preoccupied, or callously disregarding ways. In this painting the earth is literally crumbling into a sinkhole established at the bottom of the canvas, while a comely woman, clad in a flowered bathing suit, sits posing like an old-fashioned pin-up model in a fetching cross-legged pose, toes pointing daintily downward. Behind her, four men stand (or lurk) in various positions of nonchalant disregard of the catastrophe before them. Raysse likens his meaning in this work to an event, "say, at a bus stop," where someone is being killed and the bystanders ignore it. *NOW*, he specifically points out,

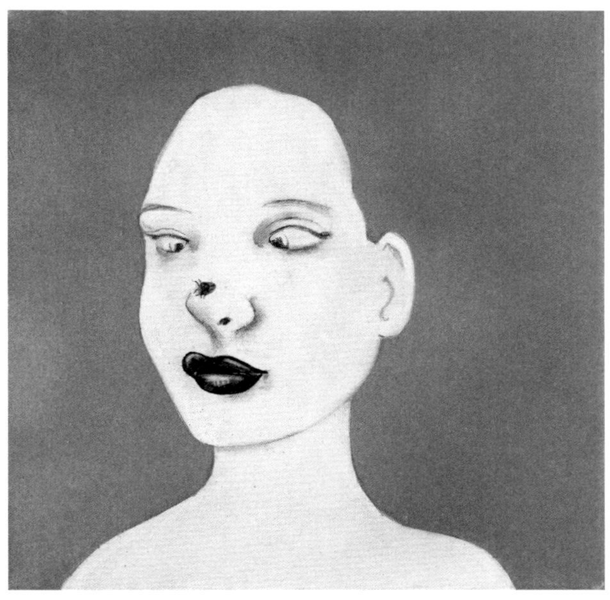

8. *Comment ça va Irma ?*, 2013. Black stone, acrylic paint and plastic ladybug on canvas, 29 ¹⁵⁄₁₆ × 28 ¾ inches (76 × 73 cm). Collection Martial Raysse

refers to our contemporary condition of "hard-heartedness." Like most of his larger compositions (and many of his smaller works), this painting was five years in the making. (He says he usually works on several paintings simultaneously, returning to any given piece numerous times, often revisiting them years later.) Every detail in a painting like this carries associations for the artist, and it follows that the viewer needs time to access it. For example, one of the men in this composition wears a red button on his sweater; though he holds out a flower to the seated woman, the button reads "NO." To further complicate the iconography in this work, Raysse has placed the entire scene in front of a barrier—a wall-sized canvas, drawn as an all-over "modern" composition—establishing the intentionally hot-house character of the space, or stage, in which the characters are set. Repeatedly encountered in Raysse's work, this device is no accident: the artist has said that for him, "space in painting is like a backdrop."

So many invented visual and literary devices appear in Raysse's works that locating them and parsing their meaning is worthy of several advanced degrees. One such device can be found in two of the pictures in this exhibition,

NOW and *QUOI ! VAN RIJN NON NON VAN DEN EECKHOUT*, (2017; page 47). In both paintings, a drawing or another painting is pinned to a virtual wall in a background plane of the picture. Close examination reveals trompe l'oeil pins affixing sheets of paper or canvas, displaying drawing or painting in styles that differ broadly from the main event. The classically beautiful woman in *QUOI ! VAN RIJN* is posed in near-profile, face lovingly modeled, rich brown hair long and lush. As though to disrupt the serene loveliness of this portrait, Raysse places a gaudy, stylized butterfly earring on her, in two shades of neon orange, grabbing the third dimension of the picture plane and rendering the entire object proto-Surreal. But another element changes the entire equation: behind the sinuously limned woman, in a recessive picture plane, we glimpse a frieze-like drawing, visible on the figure's left and right, that is pinned to a "wall"—the blue painterly ground. And on this "pinned-up" sheet are vaguely discernible fragments of Renaissance-style figure drawing, apparently unfinished, as though an Old Master had been working away in the studio when the woman arrived to pose for her portrait. The work's title now takes on concrete denotation. Its maker's intentions, at once ambiguous and legible, arrive in stages as we contemplate the painting and its title. And we discover that, at least in some of the artist's works, the title is integral to the viewer's act of appreciating the work.

Martial Raysse lives and works on the same ancient and isolated plot of ground where he settled in the early 1970s, in the bucolic countryside near Bergerac. Now in his early eighties, he appears to find himself in life pretty much where he wishes to be. He resides with his wife, the accomplished painter Brigitte Aubignac, in a complex of old stone structures, whose slow restoration for the purposes of modern living and working barely reveals the long and patient labors of their owners. The abode amid its fields and vineyards is ineffably pleasing, neither decorative nor austere. The living spaces, with their plastered walls and wood beams, and the large, rectangular studio, with its north-light-oriented skylights and high windows, reflect their inhabitants' urbane yet entirely unpretentious taste. Raysse's removal from the distractions of city living, or even easy proximity to the conveniences of a village, signals his long-ago choice to extract himself from the dialectical fray of current art discourse, and of anything more than necessary commercial dealings. He has traveled widely, usually in pursuit of the great museums and monuments of the world's civilizations, but he does not drive and prefers to communicate via the postal services whose days may be numbered. He is physically and intellectually vigorous, and steadfastly engaged in adding to his already prolific oeuvre. Having attained a satisfactory level of worldly comfort, he remains as firmly detached from the blandishments of wealth and acquisitiveness as he was when, in his thirties, he decisively abjured their pull. And yet his art is pungently redolent of the issues and facts of his own time. In some ultimately mysterious manner he has absorbed and reconstituted a language and a sensibility that belong, inextricably, to the twenty-first century. By making a decision to explore the past as inspiration for his creativity, he has found the freedom to make his own way. In his words, "what I like in art is something timeless. I like art that is local, of its place. And I can enjoy bad painting, I can learn from everything. Good painting tells us that there are many solutions.... But always, a painting should be self-explanatory." But ought we to comprehend the poetics of the painting and its title as well? Few contemporary artists would pose this conundrum with such exigency. And in this unanswerable question, he is surely correct to insist that he is a "poet above all."

1. Unless otherwise cited, all quotations from the artist are from conversation with the author, January 3, 2018.

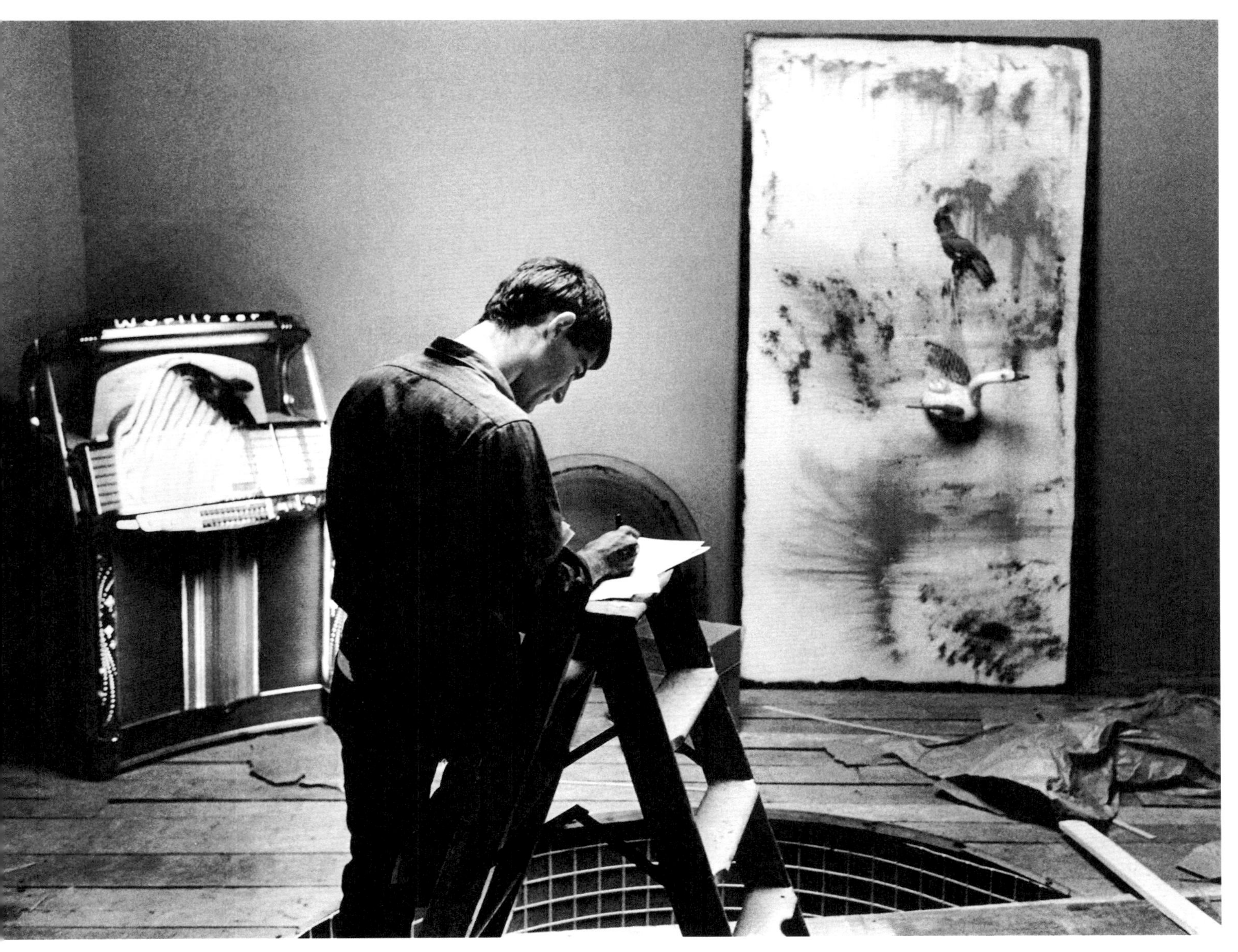

Raysse during the installation of *Dynamisch Labyrinth* (known as *Dylaby*), Stedelijk Museum, Amsterdam, 1962

Promenade avec vue sur Bacchus, le pain et le vin

MAISON DES ARTS GEORGES POMPIDOU, CAJARC

QUOI, GAYS OYSEAUS, FOLS ESPOYRS !

Le vieil homme versait une partie de sa coupe sur ce marbre où avait marché Alexandre. « Pour les dieux » disait-il. Ce geste, ces paroles, m'ont suivi longtemps. Jusqu'à cette estrade où jouaient des enfants au soir de la fête des vendanges. Par la dispute autour d'une poupée, que chacun pensait tirer à soi, une théophanie rudimentaire se montra. Ornés qu'ils étaient encore ces enfants des oripeaux de la fête.[1]

« Il prit ensuite une coupe et après avoir rendu grâces, il la leur donna en disant buvez en tous car ceci est mon sang, le sang de l'alliance. »[2]

L'eau des profondeurs se transforme en sang, le blé s'enterre et renaît, la chair, le pain et le vin.

« Un rouget grillé sur des charbons et un petit muge pêché dans le port. Voilà, Artémis, le présent que je t'apporte, moi, Ménis le pêcheur, après avoir, pour toi, repli jusqu'au bord cette coupe de vin pur et rompu ce morceau de pain sec C'est une bien pauvre offrande ; mais en échange, fais que mes filets soient toujours chargés de butin ; car c'est à toi déesse qu'appartiennent tous les rets. »[3]

perle jolie du savoir sous les si de sagesse,

« Grisé non point par le vin pourpre
Ce vin ne remplit que la coupe de la passion
Echanson venu pour servir le vin
Ne suis-je cet homme ivre d'un vin caché. »[4]

feu caché au creux des pierres.

« Oui le feu est la source de tout, voilà pourquoi le vin est sacré.
Aussi Bacchus n'est-il pas le dieu des ivrognes, mais bien le saint patron des étincelles.[5]
Au banquet des noces du printemps s'il remplit sa coupe de quelques larmes, dans l'allégresse générale elles semblent des perles. »[6]

MARTIAL RAYSSE
janvier 1997

1. Bien sûr les enfants qu'il faut au matin faire les ablutions eau bienheureuse ! eau du bonheur ! eau ! eau ! eau ! en s'aspergeant le visage à chaque fois, et boire un bon verre de jus de raisin comme le petit Bacchus du tableau, et puisque je suis dans le conseils veuillez bien saluer les premiers, car comme le dit Rabbi MATTIYAH BEN'HARACH : « sois toujours le premier à saluer tout le monde ! Mieux vaut être le dernier parmi les lions, que le premier parmi les renards ».

2. Matthieu 26 : 26.28

3. Anthologie Palatine livre VI APOLLONIDAS. 105

4. RUBÂ'YÂT DJALÂL-OD-DÎN RÛMI IVRESSE

5. BACCHUS NE BOIT PAS ! C'est une image de la juste mesure. L'ivresse bacchique n'est qu'une allusion à l'ivresse prophétique, les bacchantes jeûnent avant les cérémonies, leur ivresse vient de la danse (cf. les derviches tourneurs).

« In vino veritas » certes à condition de ne pas vider la bouteille, d'où les libations !...

Quelques décennies avant les guerres médiques, le culte des dieux du monde pluraliste d'Homère, décline au profit de la notion d'un dieu unique, Dyonisos l'esprit pur[7] Porté par un rapsode de génie Orphée, les « mystères » célébraient à Eleusis les liens entre Perséphone la mort, et Dionysos fils de dieu, dans le mystère de la résurrection[8] Cérémonies funèbres dans le temples de marbre noir à l'automne.

Ce dieu connu des seuls initiés avait son double dans le monde ordinaire. Les immémoriales cérémonies magiques paysannes nourries de l'effroi et de l'espérance du cours des saisons voyaient au temps du vin nouveau de joyeuses processions parcourir les campagnes honorant Bacchus dieu de la végétation, avec le temps des ouï-dire sur les mystères d'Eleusis, qui conduisirent ces processions à s'étoffer d'hymnes contant la gloire, la mort et la résurrection du dieu. Jusqu'au jour où l'acteur Thespis eut l'idée de remplacer ces hymnes à la troisième personne, par un acteur qui en jouait les divers épisodes. Le théâtre était né. De là la dégénérescence du mythe s'accélère et le Bacchus romain présente déjà la face chthonienne[9] communément répandue, bacchantes lubriques, silènes ivres, pour finir, après le lamentable épisode des sabazies au IIe siècle, par la destruction des temples de Delphes à l'instigation des moines ariens d'Alaric.

C'est à la Renaissance que Bacchus réapparaît, mythe christique, rédempteur déchiré par les titans pour avoir voulu sauver Perséphone, l'âme humaine, il est, pour les savants de l'époque, le témoin messianique de l'antique promesse réalisée par Jésus-Christ[10] Ainsi du *Bacchus* de Vinci voilà un tableau symbolique ; tous les véritables tableaux sont symboliques... Le but de la peinture, c'est de saisir d'une manière sensible une réalité immatérielle. Symbolon, en grec, est un signe de reconnaissance : dans un tableau se trouve un ensemble de signes à reconnaître. L'émotion, que la sensibilité et le savoir faire du peintre génèrent, ne doit pas avoir pour but de susciter chez le spectateur l'écho d'un fantasme particulier mais bien de le porter à l'esprit éveillé. A savoir : vivre l'évidence qu'il existe toujours un savoir supérieur qu'il est bénéfique de connaître. Pourquoi cette main vers le sol[11] mort ? Pourquoi l'autre main montre le ciel, résurrection ? Pourquoi cette physionomie étrange, l'androgyne primordial ? Pourquoi l'ours ? Pourquoi la peau de bête tachetée[12] ? Pourquoi le cerf ? Pourquoi l'ancolie ? Pourquoi ? Pourquoi ? La profondeur de vos réponses vous conduira à d'autres questions, les images à d'autres images, les textes à d'autres textes comme autant de mains tendues pour votre salut. En effet, dans tous les arts, un artiste authentique, c'est un être qui s'est terriblement colleté[13] avec le mystère de l'existence, au point d'être animé du désir impérieux d'en porter témoignage. La connaissance de ces itinéraires spirituels, chemin des chemins, est la voie véritable pour trouver votre propre route.

6. M. R., "Hymne à Bacchus" *DEI, SANTIE VIANDANTI*, Bologne 1996.

7. Lié aux premiers pas de la démocratie. Apollon le dieu inflexible (Marsyas) de l'arête, l'excellence, cède la place à un dieu capable de souffrir Dionysos (Sophocle, Plutarque, Apulée, Claudien, etc.).

Pour la complexité du mythe, considérer les rapports Bacchus-Moïse (Plutarque, propos de table, entre autres) et voir les statues de Moïse de Claus Sluter et de Michel-Ange avec leurs cornes, attribut déjà des représentations de Bacchus dans l'antiquité.

8. Qu'advient-il maintenant du temple d'Isis sur l'île de Philae (le soleil au zénith tombe à la verticale, du fond des puits, voir la nuit étoilée en plein jour) ? Y était peinte une belle fresque de la résurrection d'Osiris sortant du tombeau.

9. Cf. Paul Diel, *Le symbolisme dans la mythologie grecque*.

10. Cf. Marsile Ficin (de Christiana Religione), Landino (questions camaldules), Pic de la Mirandole (Heptaples) etc.

11. Certains historiens d'art pensent que ce tableau était, à l'origine, un Jean-Baptiste transformé plus tard en Bacchus ; Bacchus, il le fut depuis le début, car sinon, que serait venue faire cette main pointée vers le sol dans un Baptiste (existant en pendant par ailleurs). Ce sont des considérations d'ordre politique qui expliquent l'apparition plus tardive des attributs apparents de Bacchus.

12. Bacchus est couvert d'une peau de chevreuil, image du temps, la peau est le ciel, les taches sont les étoiles. Dans les mystères, les fidèles déchiraient un faon tacheté, allusion au dieu déchiré par les titans (d'où les légendes des bacchantes ivres, courant les montagnes en massacrant les bêtes sauvages).

13. Delacroix, *La lutte avec l'ange*, fresque de l'église St-Sulpice, Paris.

Promenade with thoughts on Bacchus, bread, and wine

MAISON DES ARTS GEORGES POMPIDOU, CAJARC

OH, GAY BIRDS, WILD HOPES!

The old man poured part of his cup onto the marble where Alexander had walked. "For the gods," he said. His action and his words stayed with me for many years, all the way to that platform where the children played on that night they celebrated the wine harvest. When they fought over a doll, in a tug of war, a rudimentary theophany appeared, as the children still wore the faded finery from the party.[1]

"Then he took a cup, and when he had given thanks he handed it to them, saying, 'Drink from this, all of you, for this is my blood, the blood of the covenant.'"[2]

The water from the depths is transformed into blood, the wheat is buried and reborn, flesh, bread and wine.

"I, Menis the net-fisher, give to thee, Artemis of the harbor, a grilled red-mullet and a hake, a cup of wine filled to the brim with a piece of dry bread broken into it, a poor sacrifice, in return for which grant that my nets may be always full of fish; for all nets, gracious goddess, are given to thy keeping."[3]

pretty pearl of knowledge under the ifs of wisdom,

"This drunkenness of mine
Is of no crimson wine;
My wine doth not pass
Except in passion's glass.

O friend, was it thy will
With me this wine to spill?
The wine that moves my mirth
Was never seen on earth."[4]

fire hidden deep in the stones.

"Yes, fire is the source of all things, that is why wine is sacred.
That is why Bacchus is not the god of drunkards, but the patron saint of sparks.[5]
If, at spring's nuptial banquet, he fills his cup with a few tears, they will seem like pearls in the general joy."[6]

MARTIAL RAYSSE
January 1997

1. Of course, children, you must make your morning ablutions in the blessed water! The water of happiness! Water! Water! Water! Spray your face each time, and drink a good glass of grape juice like the little Bacchus in the painting, and as I'm giving advice, take care to be the first to greet, for as Rabbi MATTIYAH BEN'HARACH says: "Always be the first to greet everyone! It is better to be the last among the lions than the first among the foxes."

2. Matthew 26, 27–28.

3. Apollonides, *Palatine Anthology*, book VI, 105–108. [English translation: *The Greek Anthology*, trans. W.R. Paton (London and New York: William Heinemann and G.P. Putnam's Sons, 1916–18), 357.]

4. *The Rubāʿīyāt of Jalāl Al-Dīn Rūmī* [English translation: Jalāl Al-Dīn Rūmī, *The Rubāʿīyāt of Jalāl Al-Dīn Rūmī*. Trans. A.J. Arberry (London: Emery Walker, 1949), 60.

5. BACCHUS DOES NOT DRINK! He is an image of due measure. Bacchic drunkenness is simply an allusion to prophetic headiness. The Bacchantes fast before ceremonies; their drunkenness comes from dance (cf. the whirling dervishes).

"In vino veritas," fine, providing one does not empty the bottle. Hence libations!

A few decades before the Greco-Persian wars, the cult of the gods of Homer's pluralist world went into decline, giving way to the notion of a single god, Dionysus the pure spirit.[7] Sustained by a rhapsode of genius, Orpheus, the "Eleusinian Mysteries" celebrated the bonds between Persephone, death, and Dionysus the son of god, in the mystery of resurrection.[8] Funeral ceremonies were held in autumn in temples of black marble.

This god known only to initiates had his double in the ordinary world. The immemorial magical ceremonies of the peasants nourished by dread and hope over the course of the seasons, saw joyous processions pass through the countryside honoring Dionysus, god of vegetation, in the time of new wine, with the time of hearsay about the Eleusinian mysteries, which led these processions to be enriched with hymns singing of the glory, death and resurrection of the god. Until one day the actor Thespis had the idea of replacing these hymns in the third person with an actor who would play the various episodes. Theater was born. Now the degeneration of the myth accelerated and the Roman Bacchus already has that now-common chthonic face.[9] Now come the lubricious bacchantes, the drunken sileni, ending up with the lamentable episode of the sabazia in the second century and, after that, the destruction of the temples in Delphi at the instigation of Alaric's Aryan monks.

Bacchus reappears in the Renaissance in a Christ myth, as a redeemer torn apart by the Titans for having tried to save Persephone, the human soul. For learned commentators at the time, he was the messianic witness to the antique promise accomplished by Jesus Christ.[10] The Leonardo da Vinci *Bacchus* is a symbolic painting; all true paintings are symbolic. The goal of painting is to capture an immaterial reality in a sensorial form. *Symbolon*, in Greek, is a sign of recognition: a painting contains a set of signs to be recognized. The point of the emotion generated by the painter's sensibility and skill must not be to arouse in the beholder the echo of a particular fantasy but, rather, to create a state of mental wakefulness. Experiencing the realization that there is always a higher knowledge that it is beneficial to know. Why this hand pointing towards the dead ground?[11] Why does the other hand show the sky, resurrection? Why this strange physiognomy, the primordial androgyne? Why the bear? Why the spotted animal skin?[12] Why the stag? Why the aquilegia? Why? Why? The depth of your answers will lead you to other questions, the images to other images, the texts to other texts, like so many hands reaching out to save you. Indeed, in all the arts, an authentic artist is a being who has grappled[13] harrowingly with the mystery of existence, so much so that he is driven by the imperious desire to bear witness to it. Knowledge of these spiritual itineraries, the path of paths, is the true way for finding your own route.

6. M. R., "Hymn to Bacchus" in Anne-Marie Sauzeau, *Enzo Chcchi – Martial Raysse, Dei, Santi e Viandanti* (Bologna: Museo Civico Medieval; Ravenne: Danilo Montanari Editore, 1996).

7. Linked to the first steps of democracy. Apollo, the inflexible god (Marsyas) of the frozen and of excellence, gives way to a god capable of suffering: Dionysus (Sophocles, Plutarch, Apuleius, Claudian, etc.).

For the complexity of the myth, consider the Bacchus-Moses relations in Claus Sluter and Michelangelo, with their horns, an attribute of Bacchus in antiquity.

8. What happens here to the temple of Isis on the island of Philae (the light of the sun at its zenith is vertical. From the bottom of the well, visions of the starry sky in broad daylight)? There was a fine fresco there showing the resurrection of Osiris as he emerges from the tomb.

9. Cf. Paul Diel, *Le symbolisme dans la mythologie grecque* (Paris: Payot, 2002).

10. Cf. Marsilio Ficino (*De Christiana Religione*), Landino (*Disputationes Camaldulenses*), Pico de la Mirandola (*Heptaplus*), etc.

11. Some art historians believe that this painting originally showed John the Baptist and was later transformed into a Bacchus, but it was surely a Bacchus right from the start: how would one explain that hand pointing down at the ground if this was a John the Baptist (especially since that painting already exists as a pendant)? It is political considerations that explain the later appearance of the visible Bacchic attributes.

12. Bacchus is covered with a deerskin, an image of time: the skin is the sky, the marks are the stars. In the mysteries, the faithful tore apart a flecked fawn, alluding to the god being torn apart by the Titans (hence the legends of drunken Bacchantes running across the mountains and massacring wild beasts).

13. Delacroix, *Jacob Wrestling with the Angel*, fresco in the church of St-Sulpice, Paris.

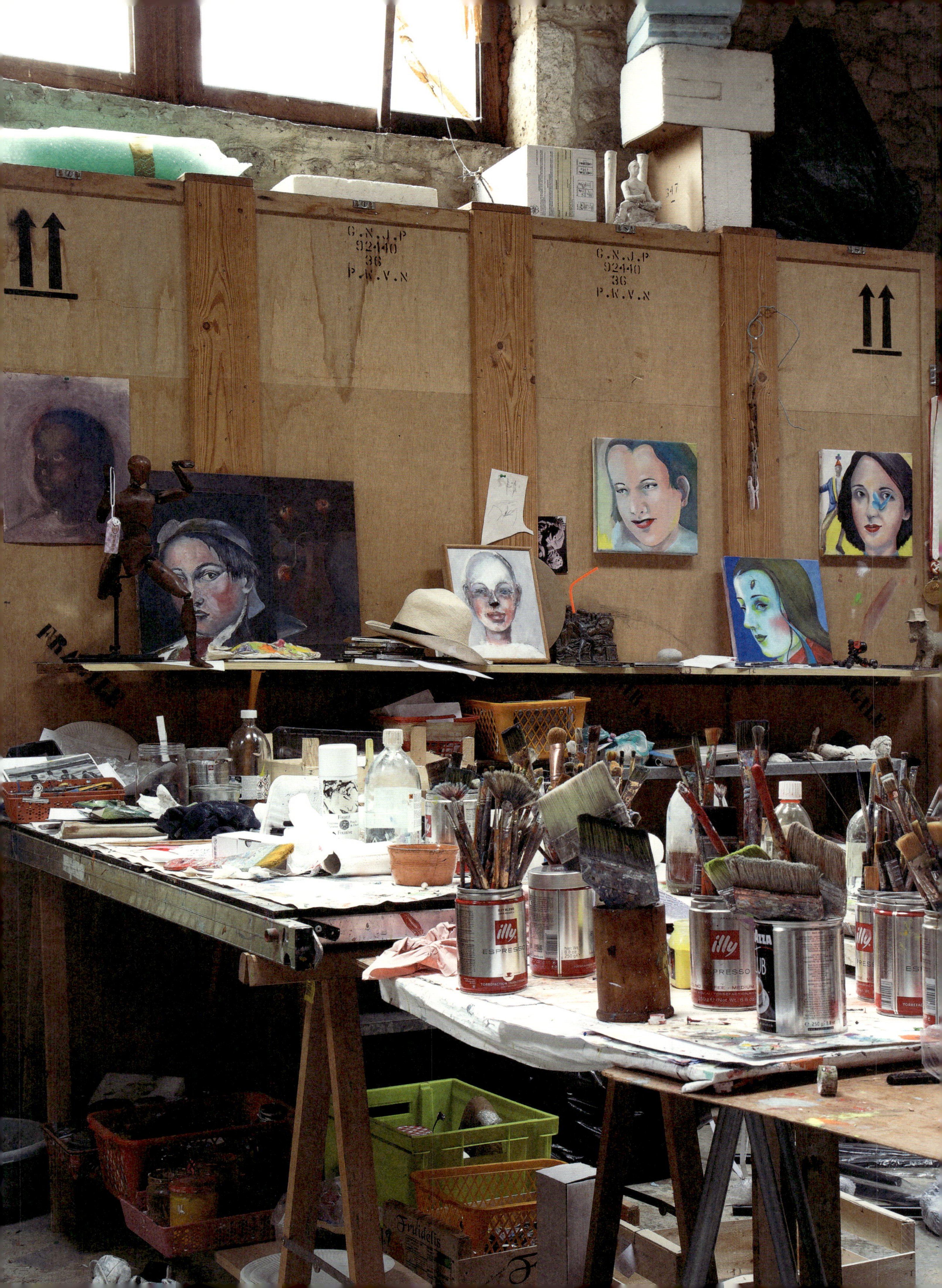
illy
ESPRESSO

MARTIAL RAYSSE: VISAGES

Un extrait de *Qu'il est long le chemin*, conférence prononcée le 13 mai 1984 au Centre Georges Pompidou

Mais existe aussi le grand travail de l'art. *Daidalein*, dissent les Grecs, Dédale est le créateur par excellence. *Daidalein*, c'est l'agencement des significations, agencement dans et par lequel celui qui est guidé par le fil d'Ariane—l'amour combatif de la vérité—trouve la sortie vers la lumière, l'accomplissement du sens éthique de la vie. L'autre erre dans ce qui reste un labyrinthe. Car n'en doutez pas, dire de la Joconde que c'est une jeune fille au sourire énigmatique ou de la Mélancolie de Dürer qu'elle représente un jeune homme triste entouré de symboles, c'est être dans le labyrinthe. Hygiène de la vision, oui, et encore, et toujours, car être moderne c'est avant tout voir plus clair. Le peintre et la peinture moderne sont à venir.

J'entends qu'on me demande « *et alors que faire ?* » Eh bien…Ce que l'on nous disait quand nous étions petits : grandir en sagesse et puis, pour ceux que cela concerne, dessiner, non pas ce dessin de silhouette ou de contour qui permet toutes les pirouettes, mais dessiner par l'ombre et la lumière. Quelle merveille, séparer la lumière des ténèbres…

Ah ! qu'il est long le chemin qui mène à ma blonde !….

An excerpt from *How the path is long*, lecture given on May 13, 1984 at the Centre Georges Pompidou

But the great labour of art also exists—the Greeks would describe it as *daedalian*. Daedalus is the creator par excellence. *Daedalian* describes the arrangement of significations, an arrangement in and through which he who is guided by Ariadne's thread—the combative love of truth—finds his way out to the light, the accomplishment of the ethical sense of life. The other wanders in what remains a labyrinth. For have no doubt, to say of the Mona Lisa that it is a young girl with an enigmatic smile, or of Dürer's Melancholia that it represents a sad young man surrounded by symbols, is to be inside the labyrinth. Cleanness of vision, yes, and more, and always, for to be modern is above all to see more clearly. The modern painter and modern painting are on their way.

I hear you ask "*so, what should we do?*" Well…what we used to be told when we were little: grow up wise and then, for those who are interested, draw—not the drawing of silhouettes or contours that allows us a lot of ambiguity, but drawing through shadow and light. How marvelous, to separate light from dark…

Oh! How long it is, the path that leads to my girl!….

MARTIAL RAYSSE

"I began my work with preexisting clichés. These clichés are commonplaces, leitmotivs of the emotional climate of an era. Since then I've been trying to create my own vocabulary, my own clichés."

—MARTIAL RAYSSE, 1992

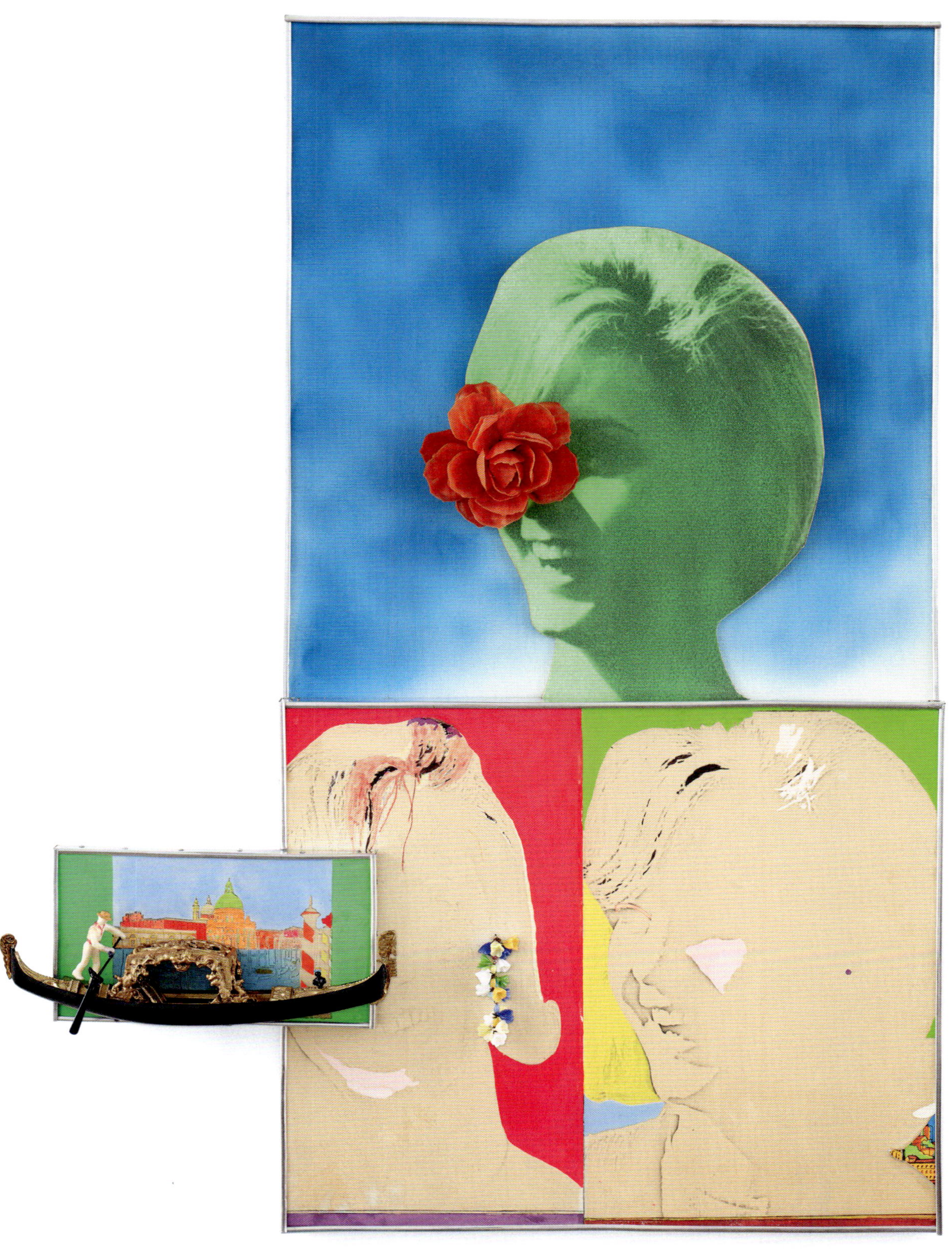

The Bird

What woman.

Marilyn e morte

permanently dead
or permanently mortal.

a harsh face chuckling
a warbling sound

scattered applause

a flap door shutting
a paper flag

OH

What woman

rolling a TV around
from room to room.

It might not be narrative
just things

happening.

Pure red and luminous red.
Cosmos pink and opera.

It reminded me
of interruption
Like being bad

Not keeping still.

Hammer noise and the people
ignoring it

I don't really know

what is going
to happen.

Inserting a look
not always listening

OH

singing, indistinct

What woman

cooking an empty pan
all night

Laughing and screaming

the naked planet

whoever she
was

a roundish face

that knew
itself

OH

Is a woman a boy against God?

I think she must be.

sunshiny
with secret corridors

hopping out
of her seat

It's political

Interruption is.

a spitty kiss
a centipede

on your car
your guitar

OH

What woman.

—LEOPOLDINE CORE

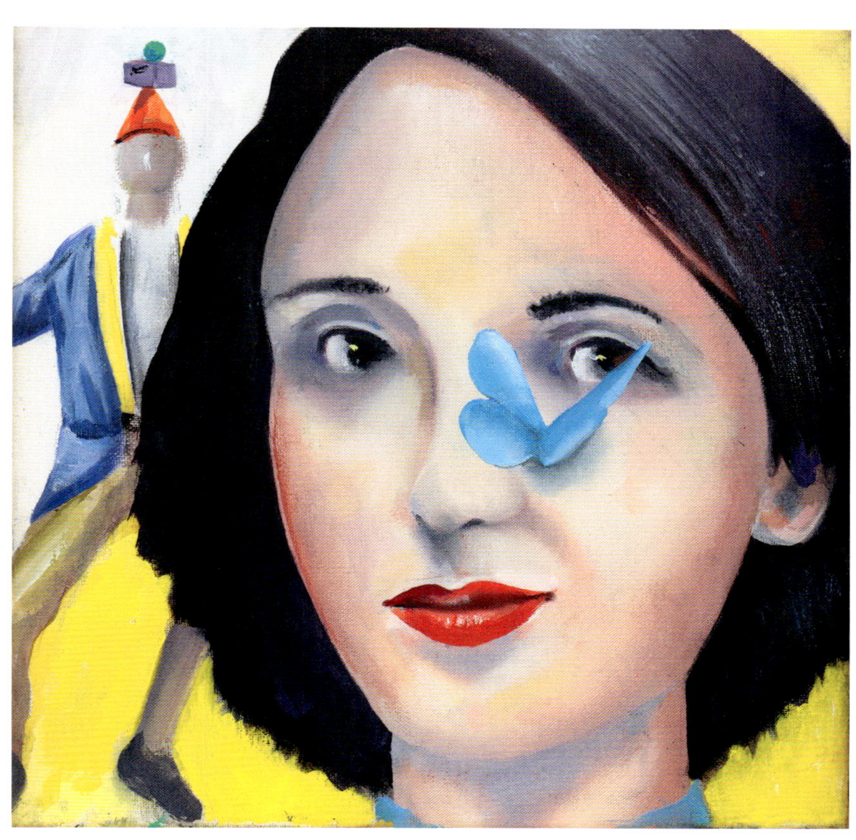

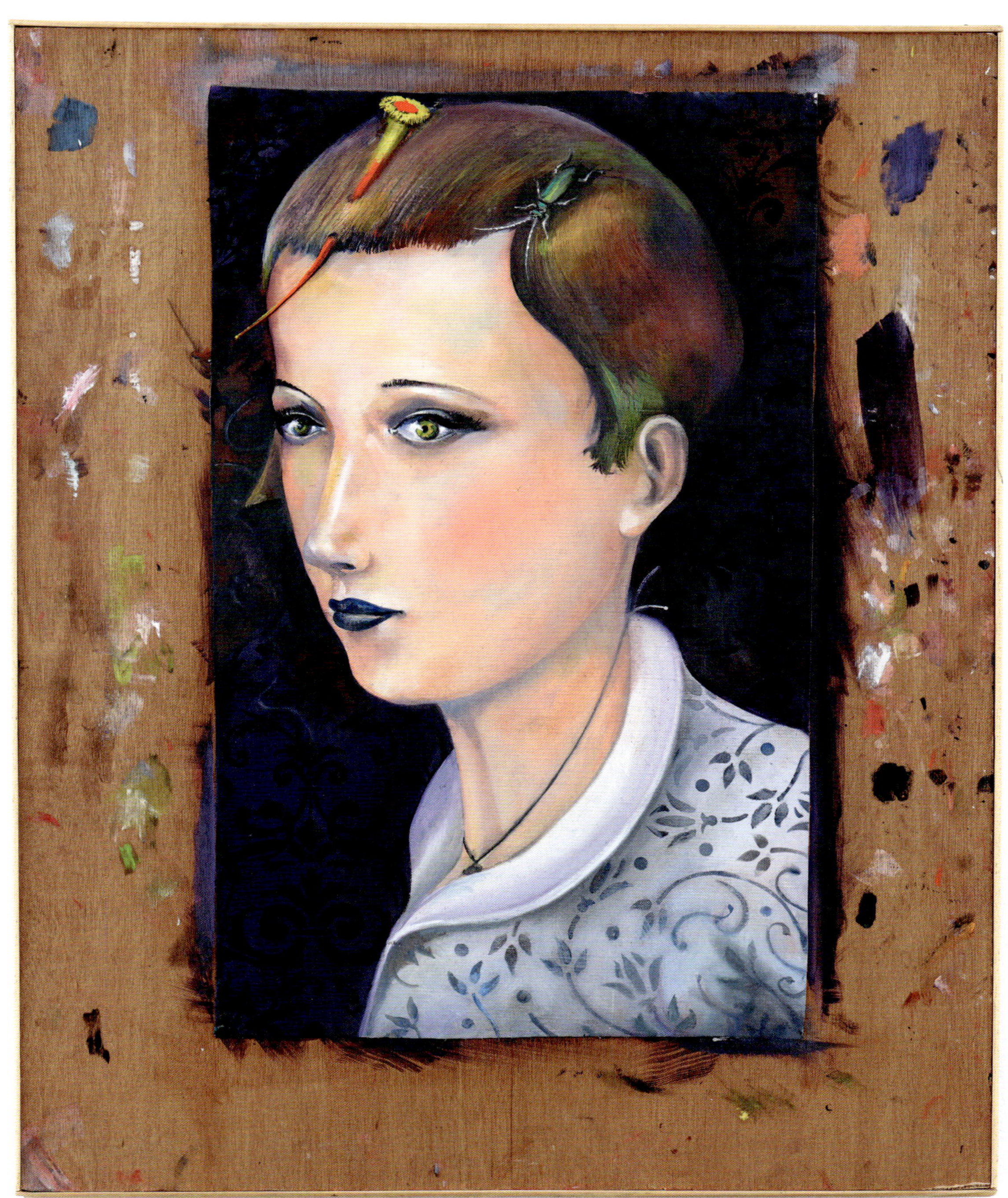

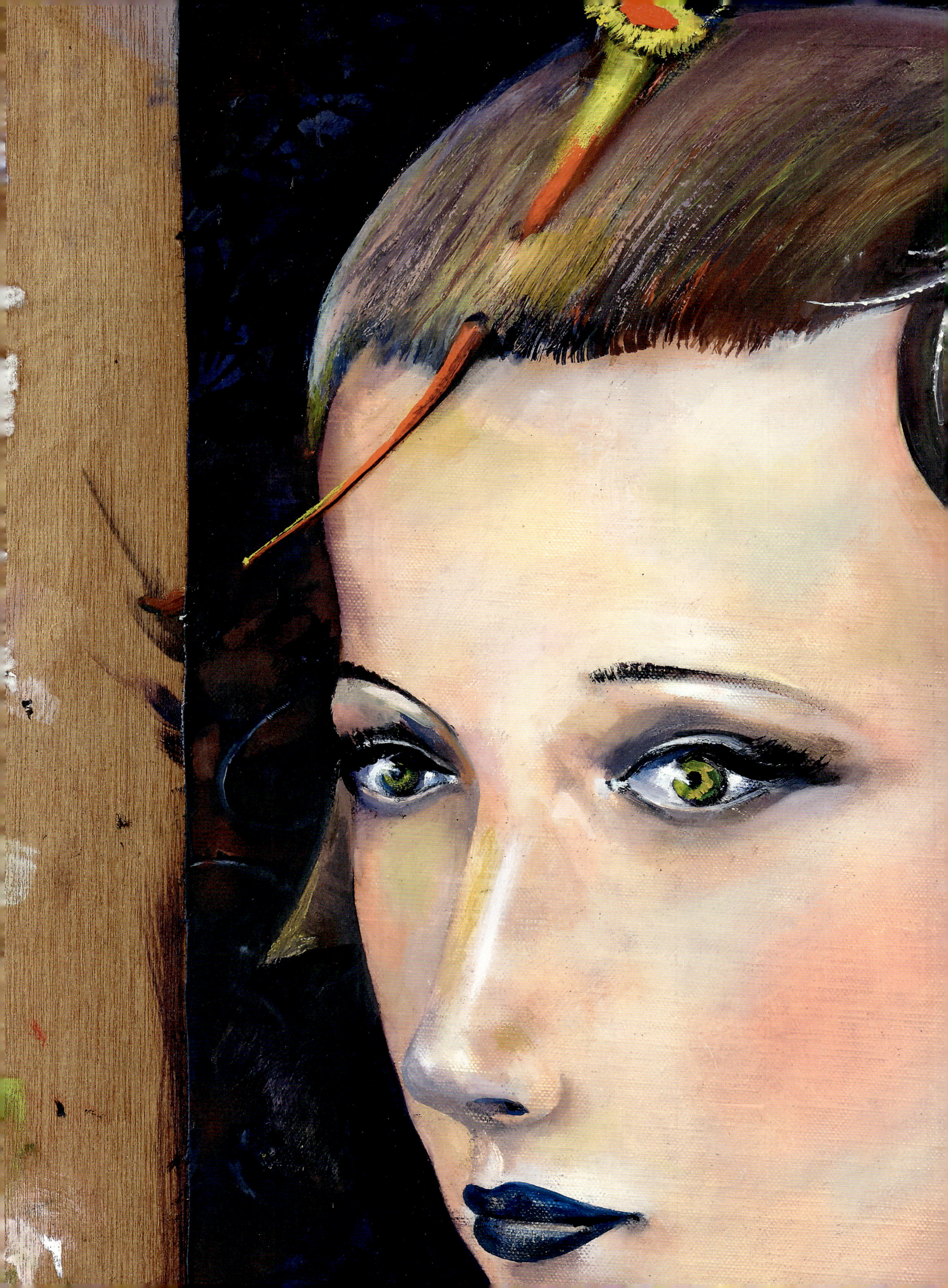

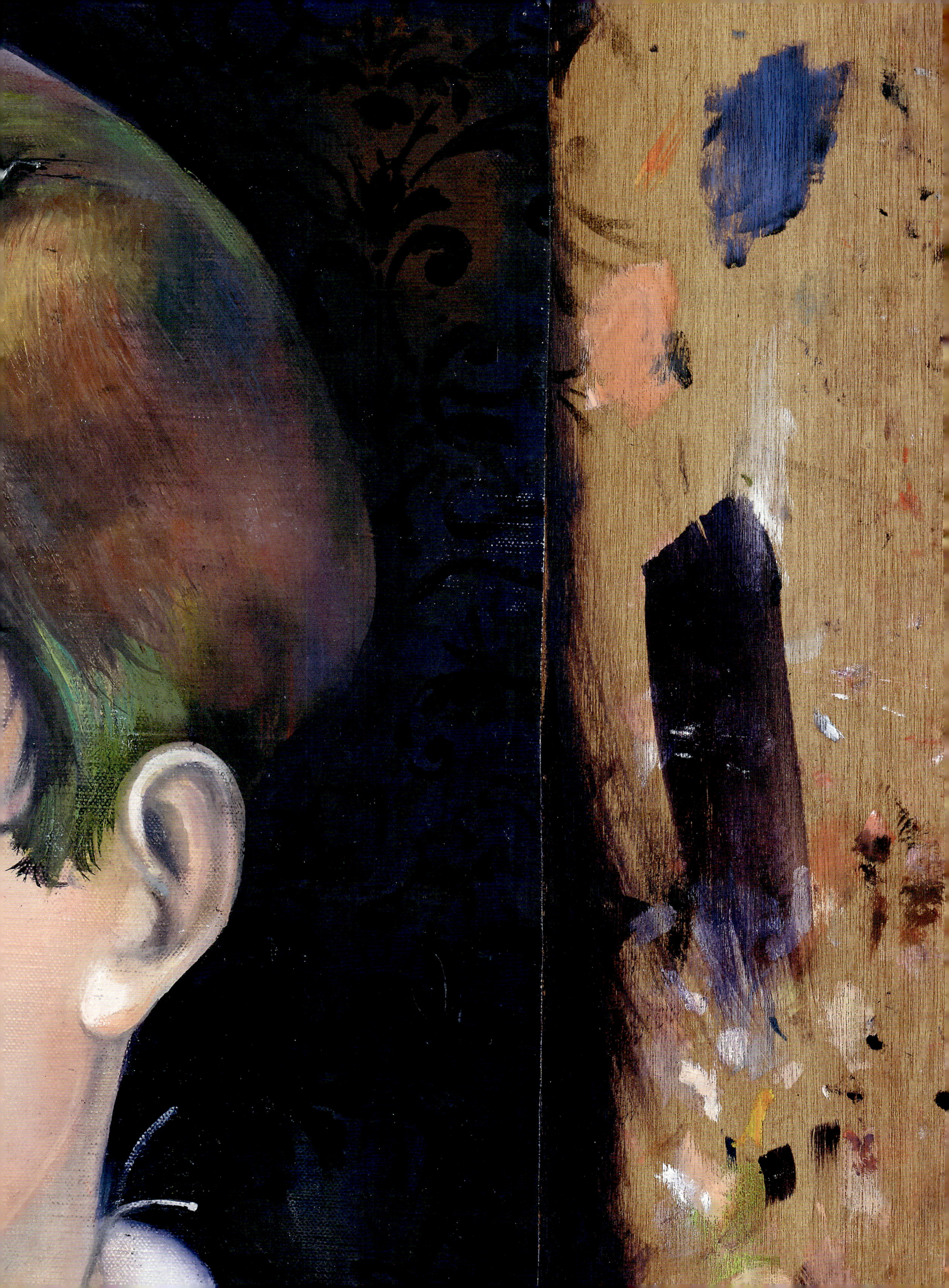

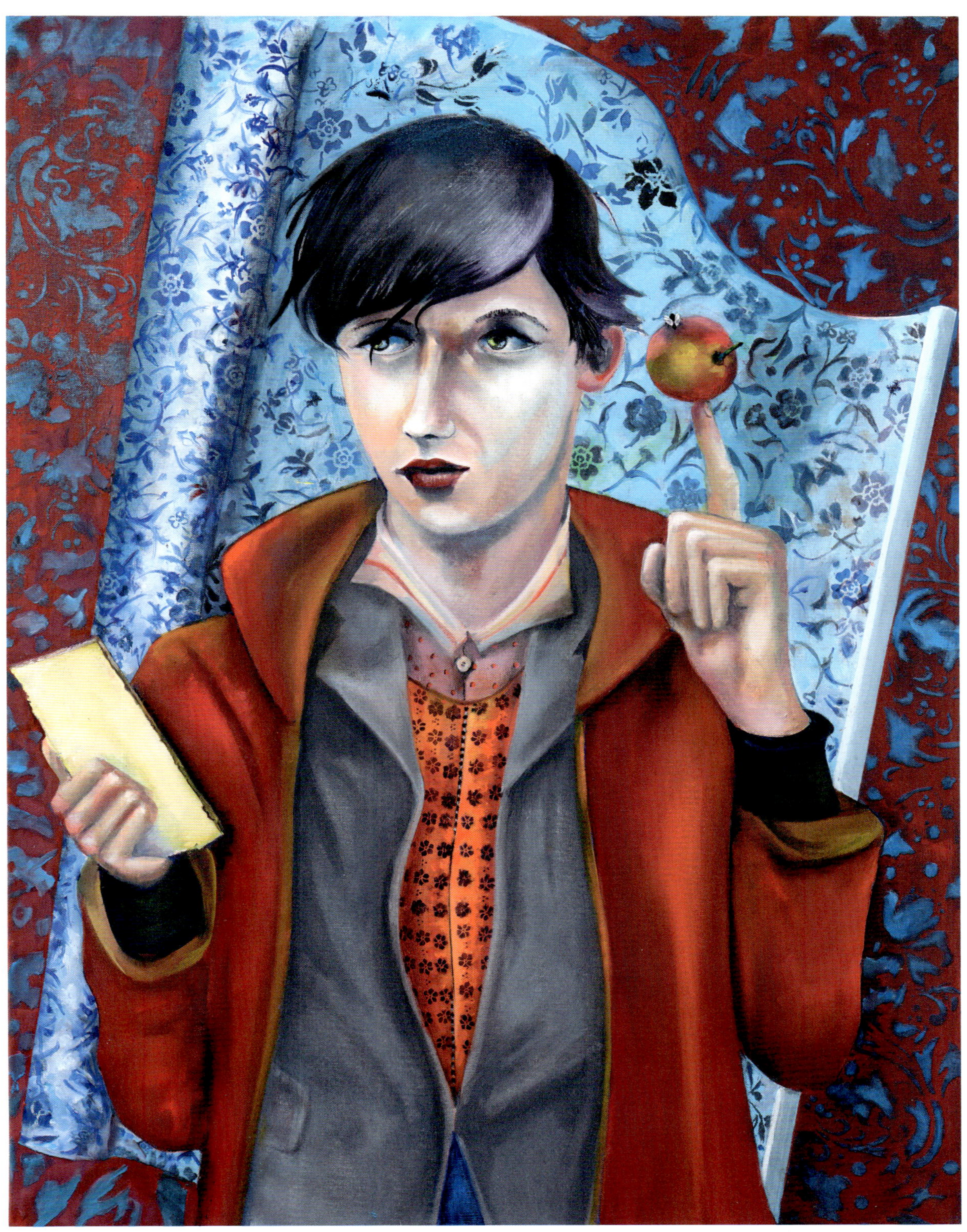

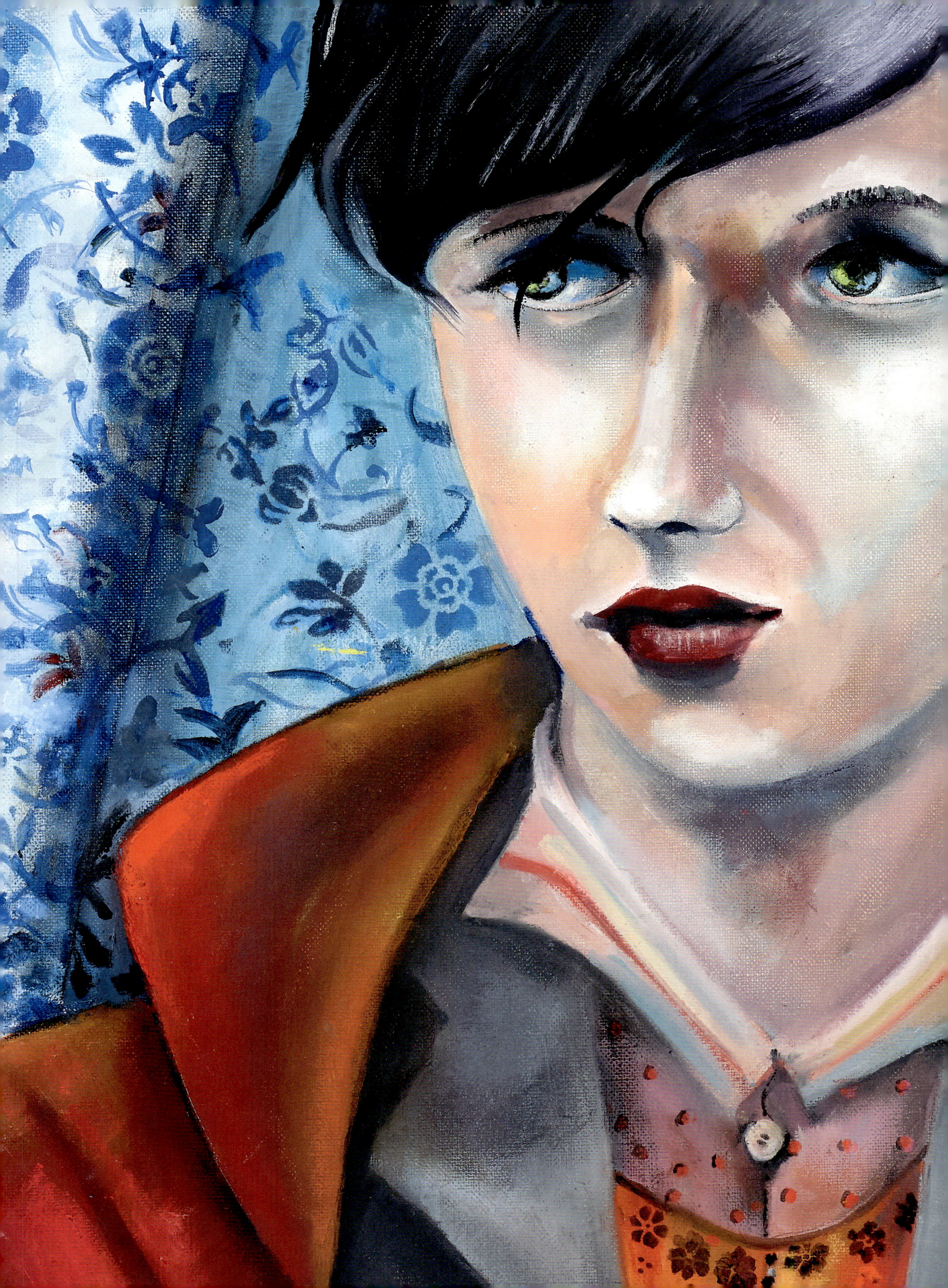

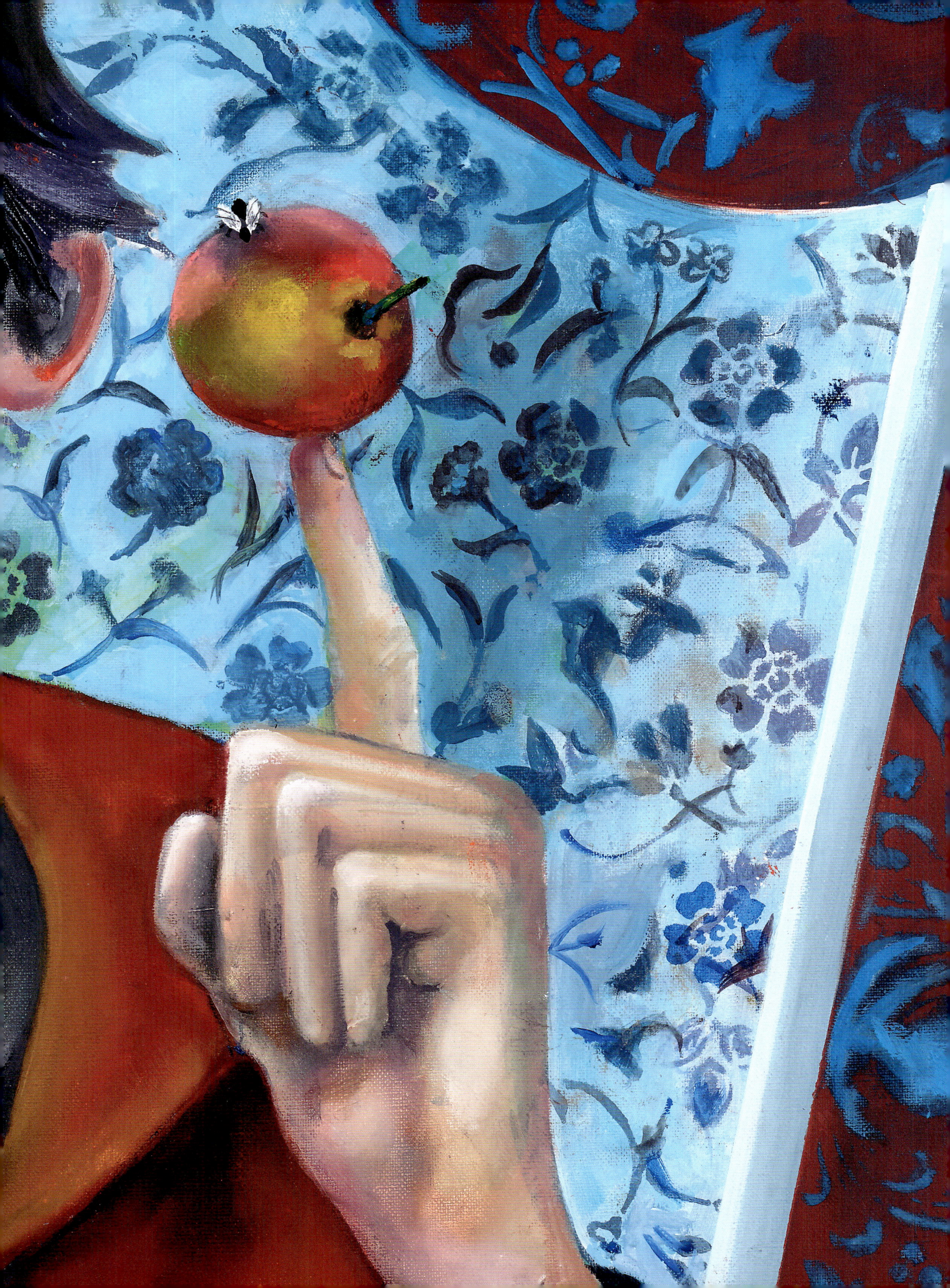

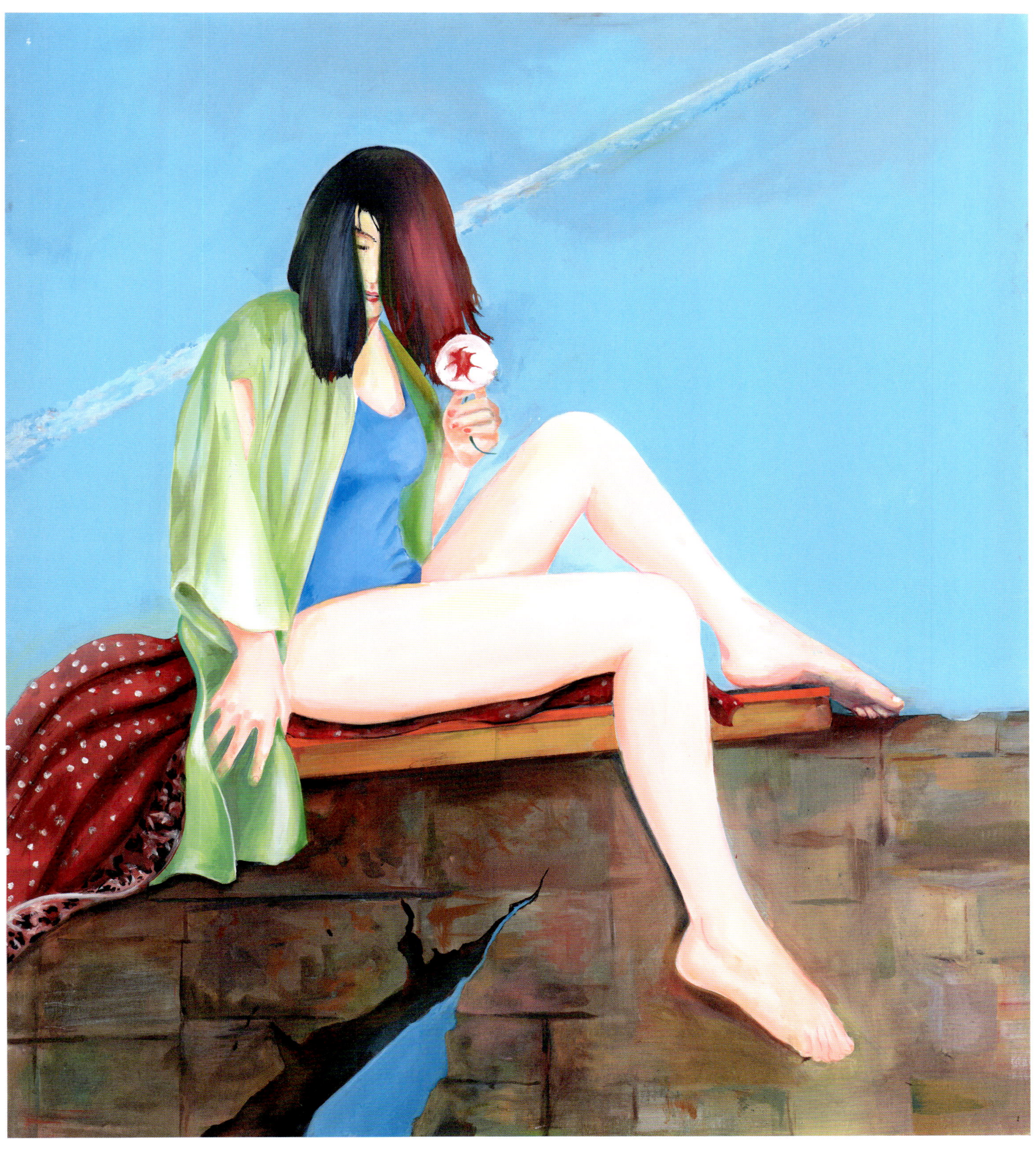

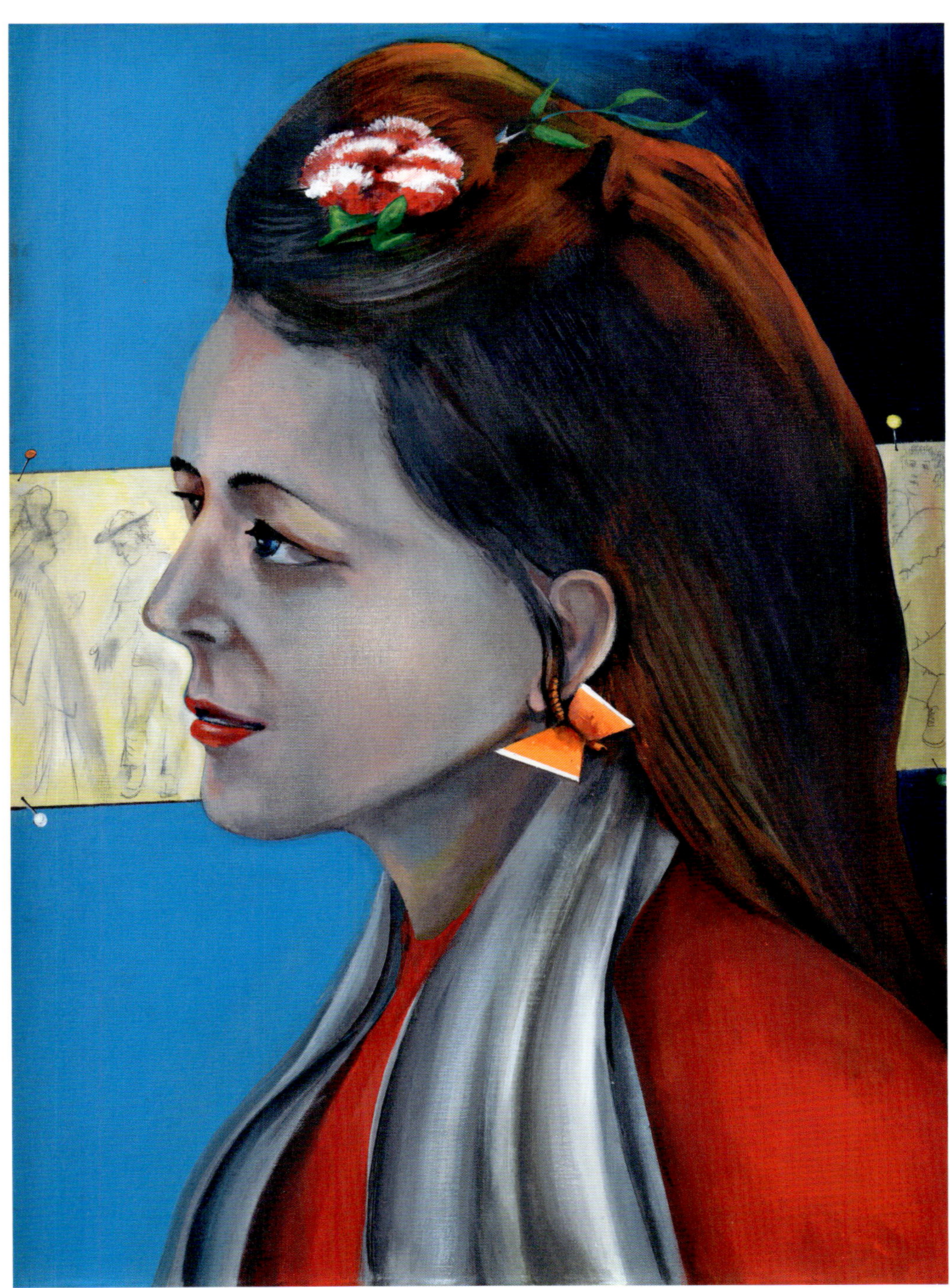

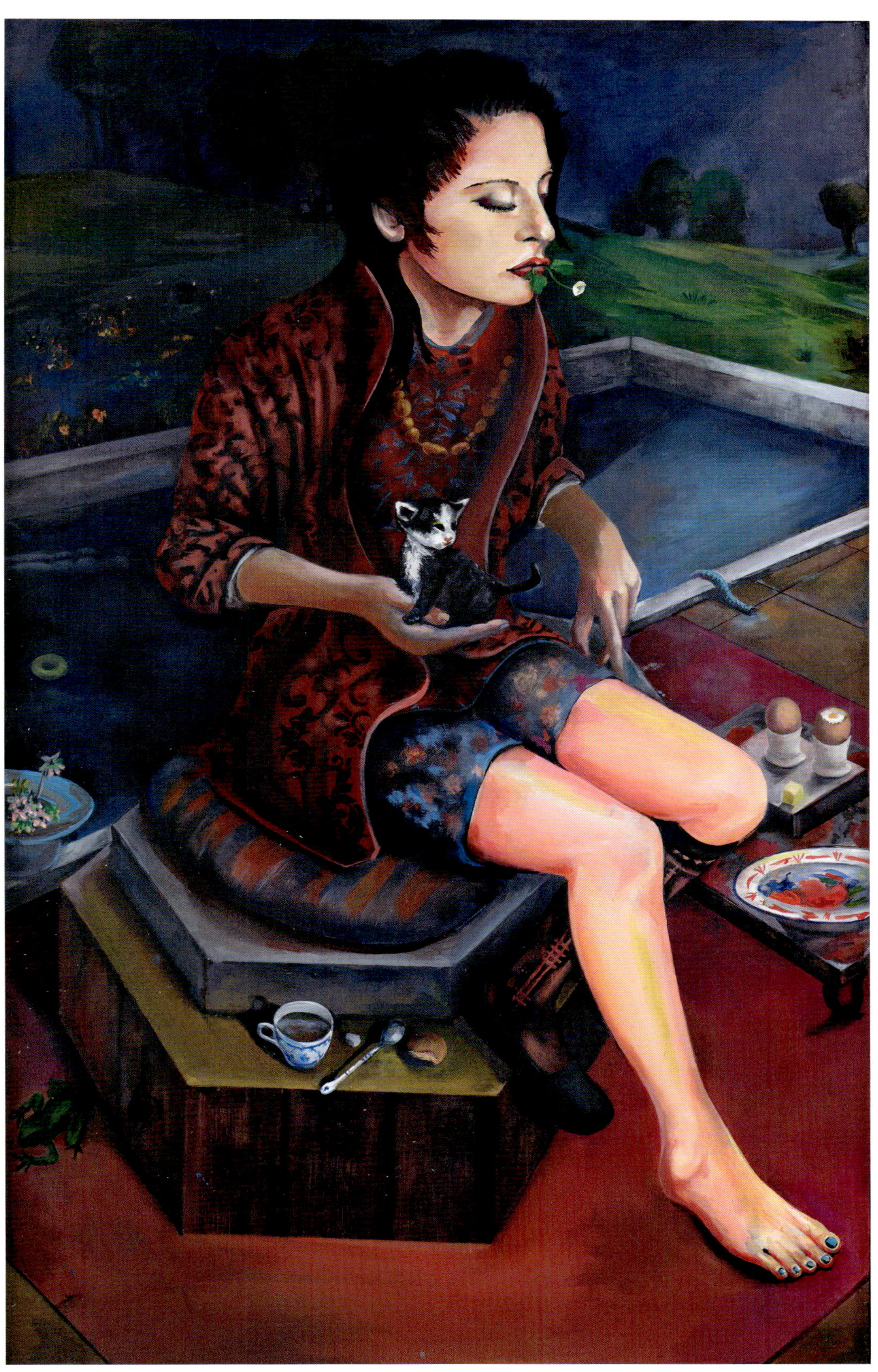

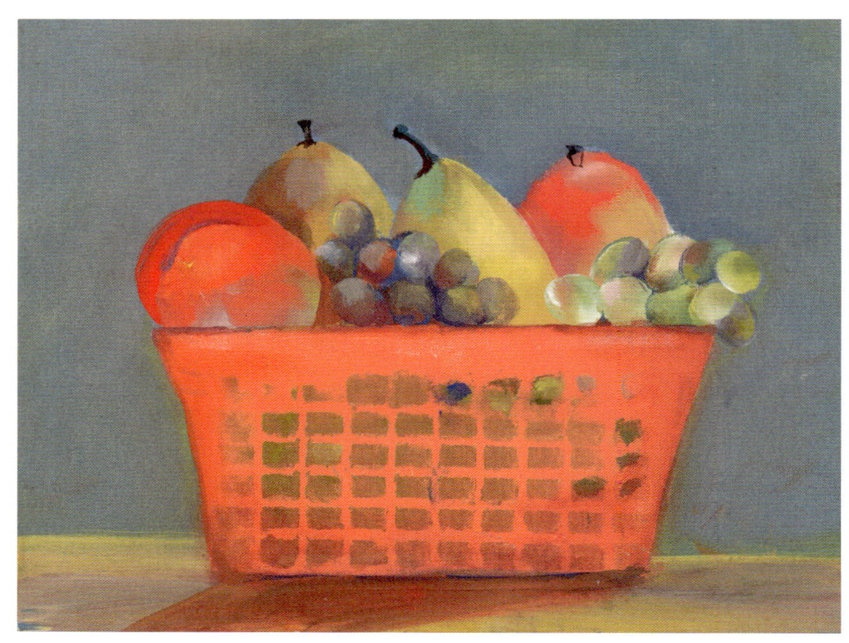

 BEL AMOUR 1998

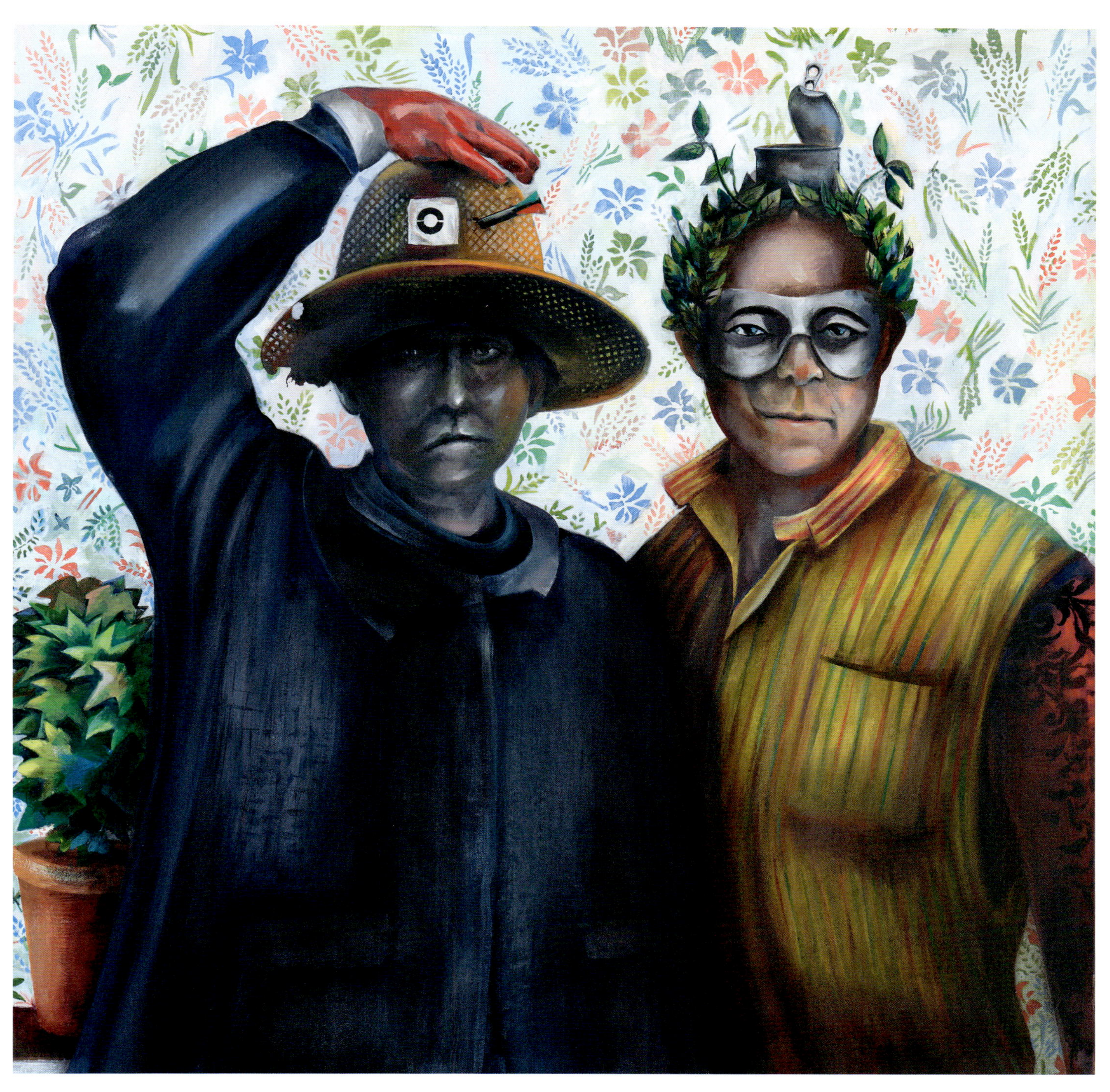

CES DEUX GARS-LÀ 2008

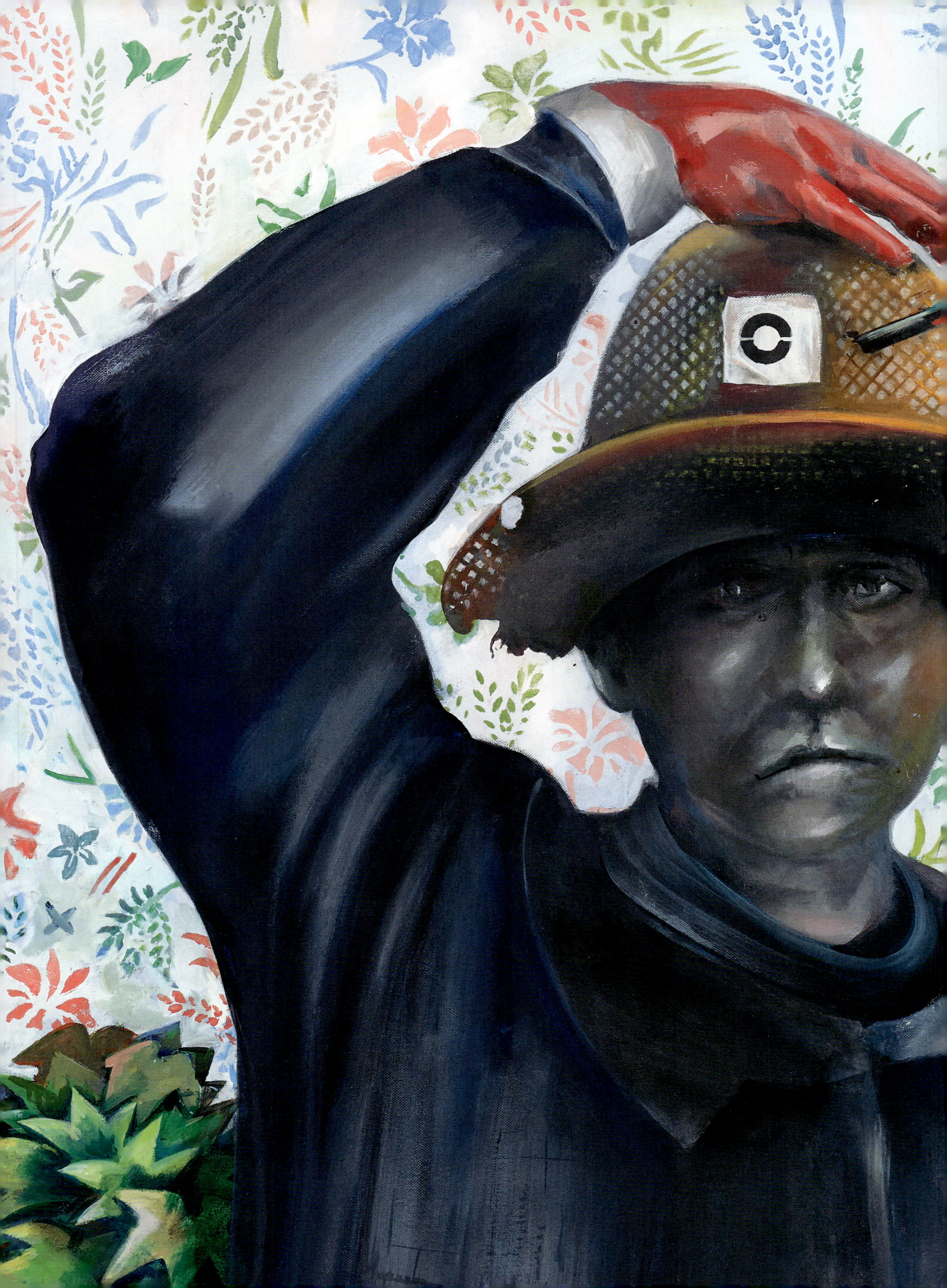

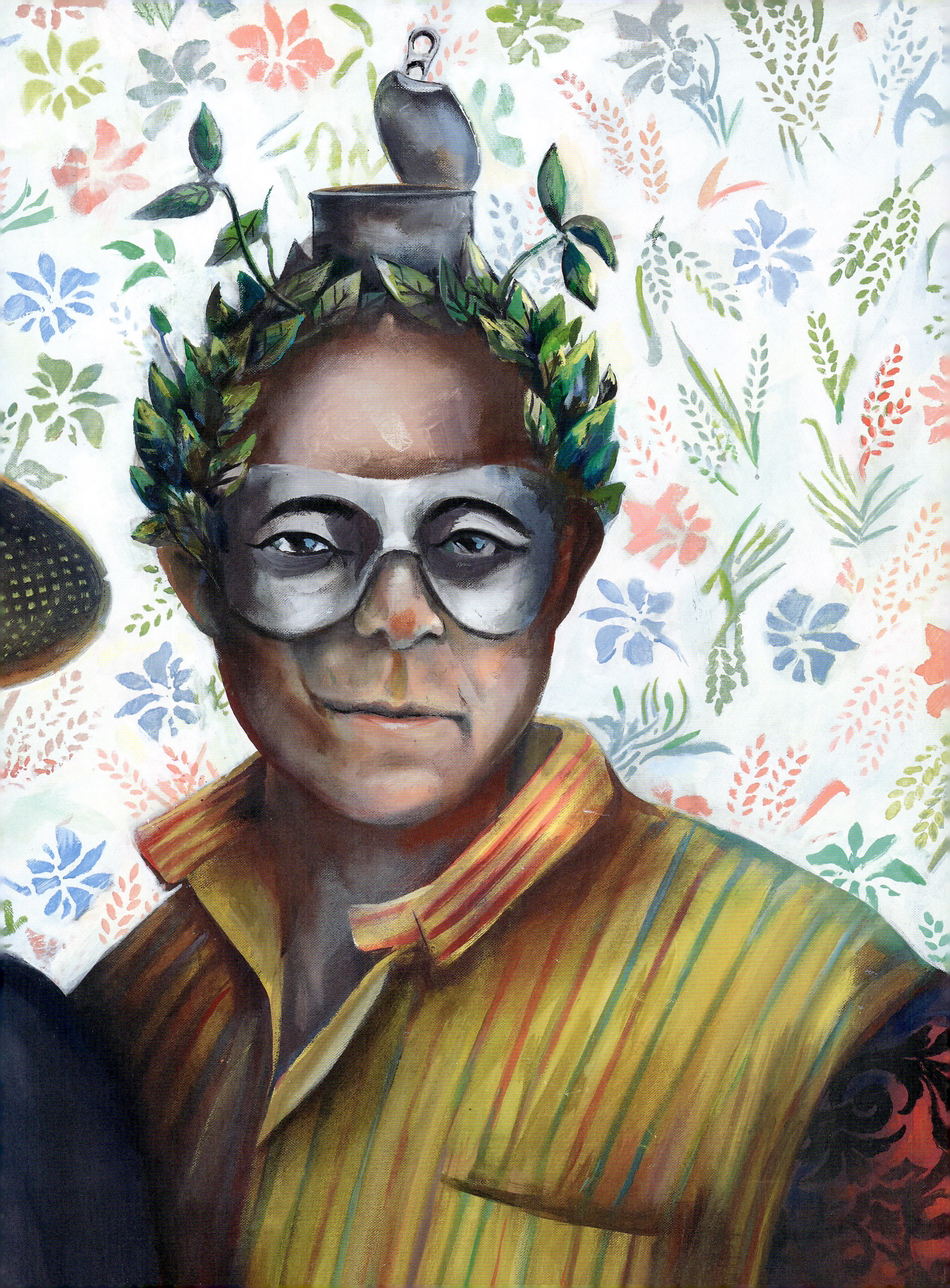

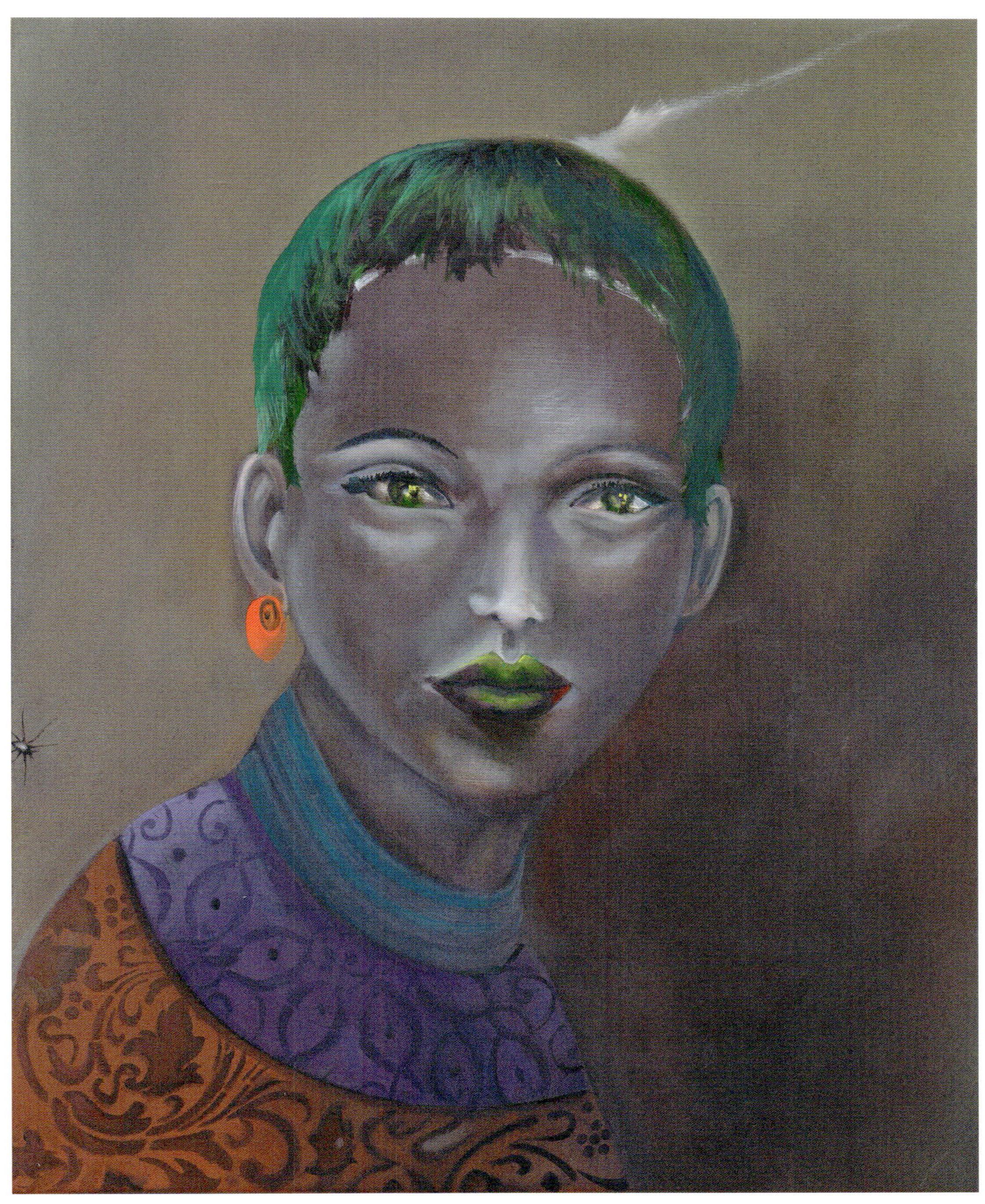

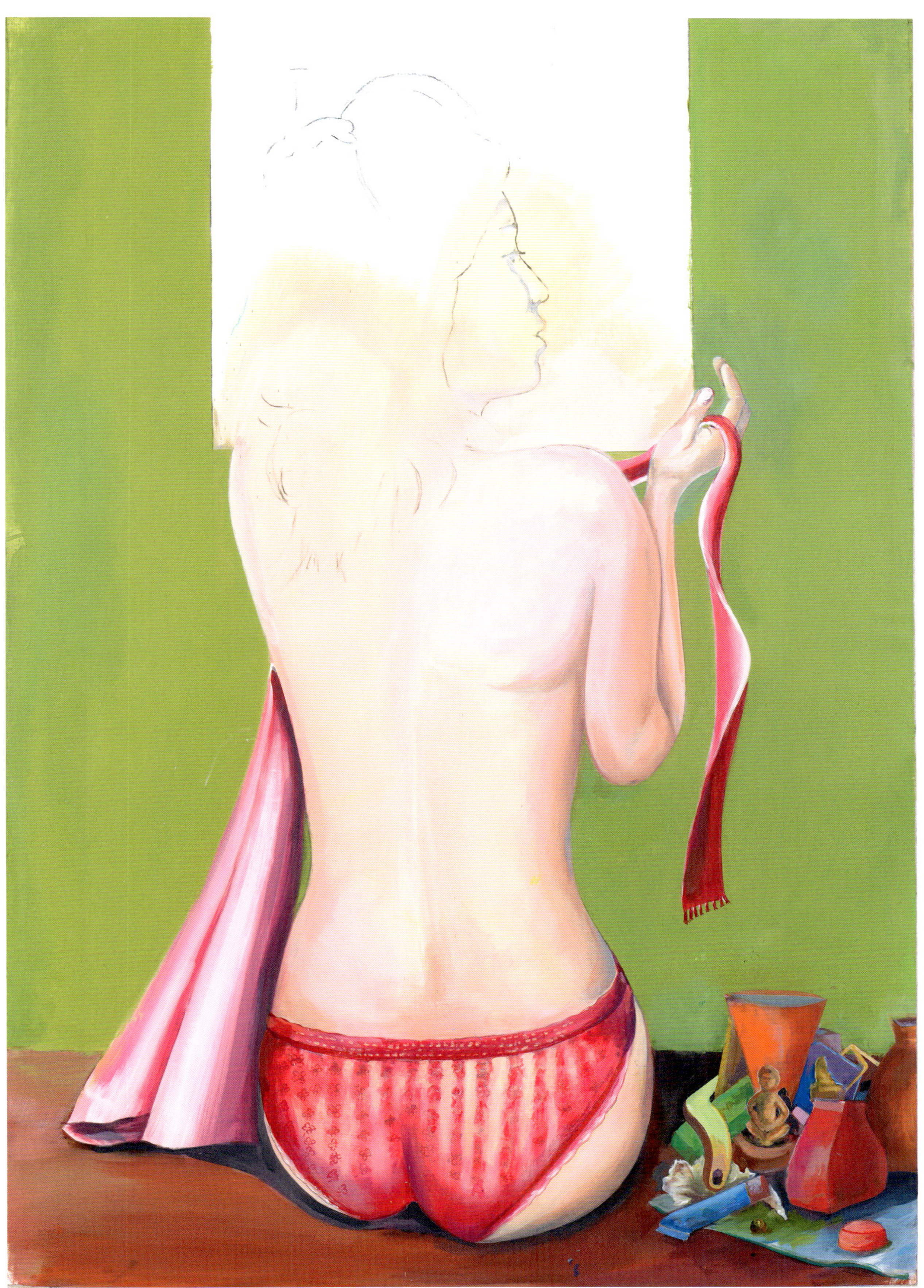

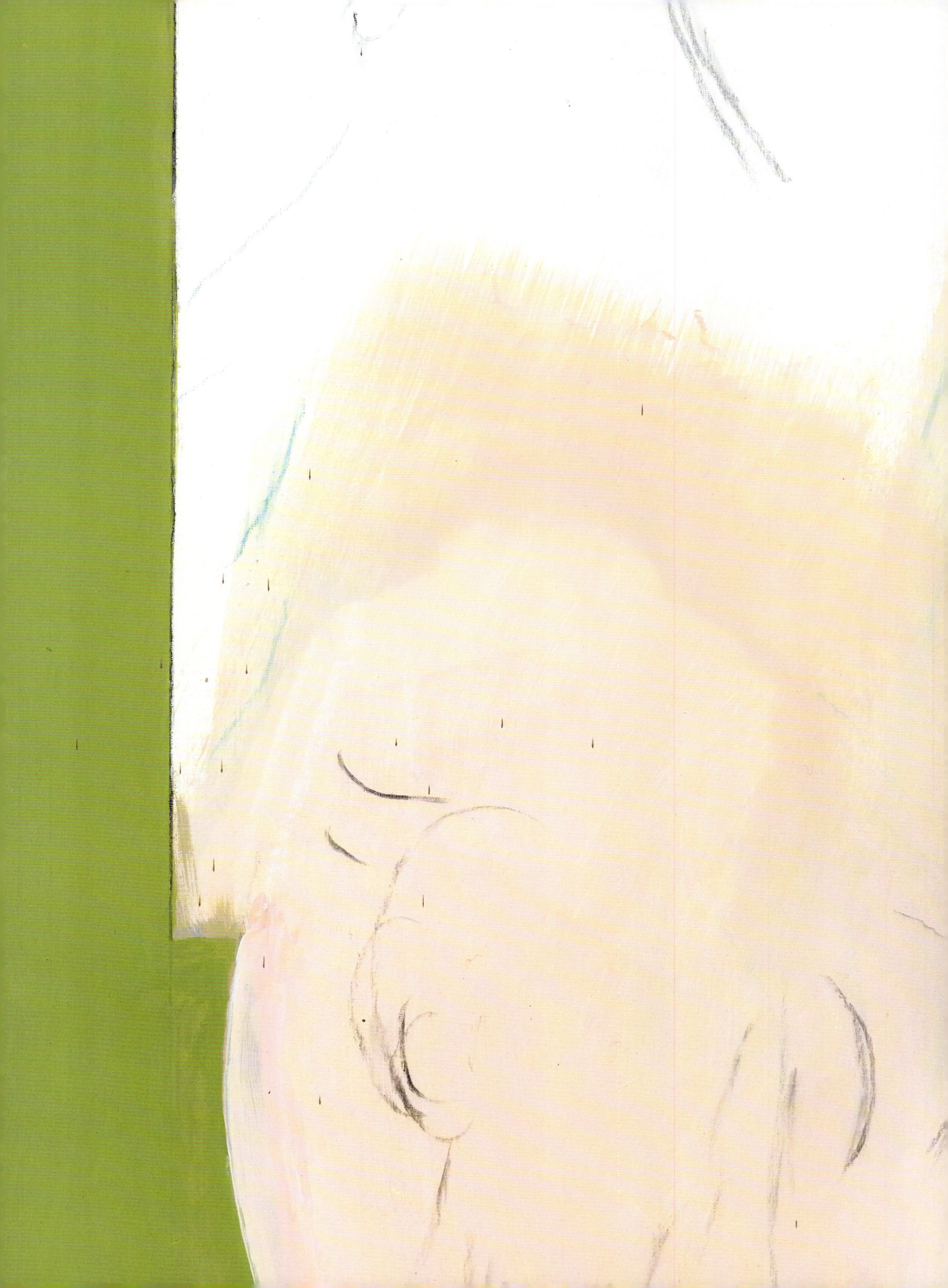

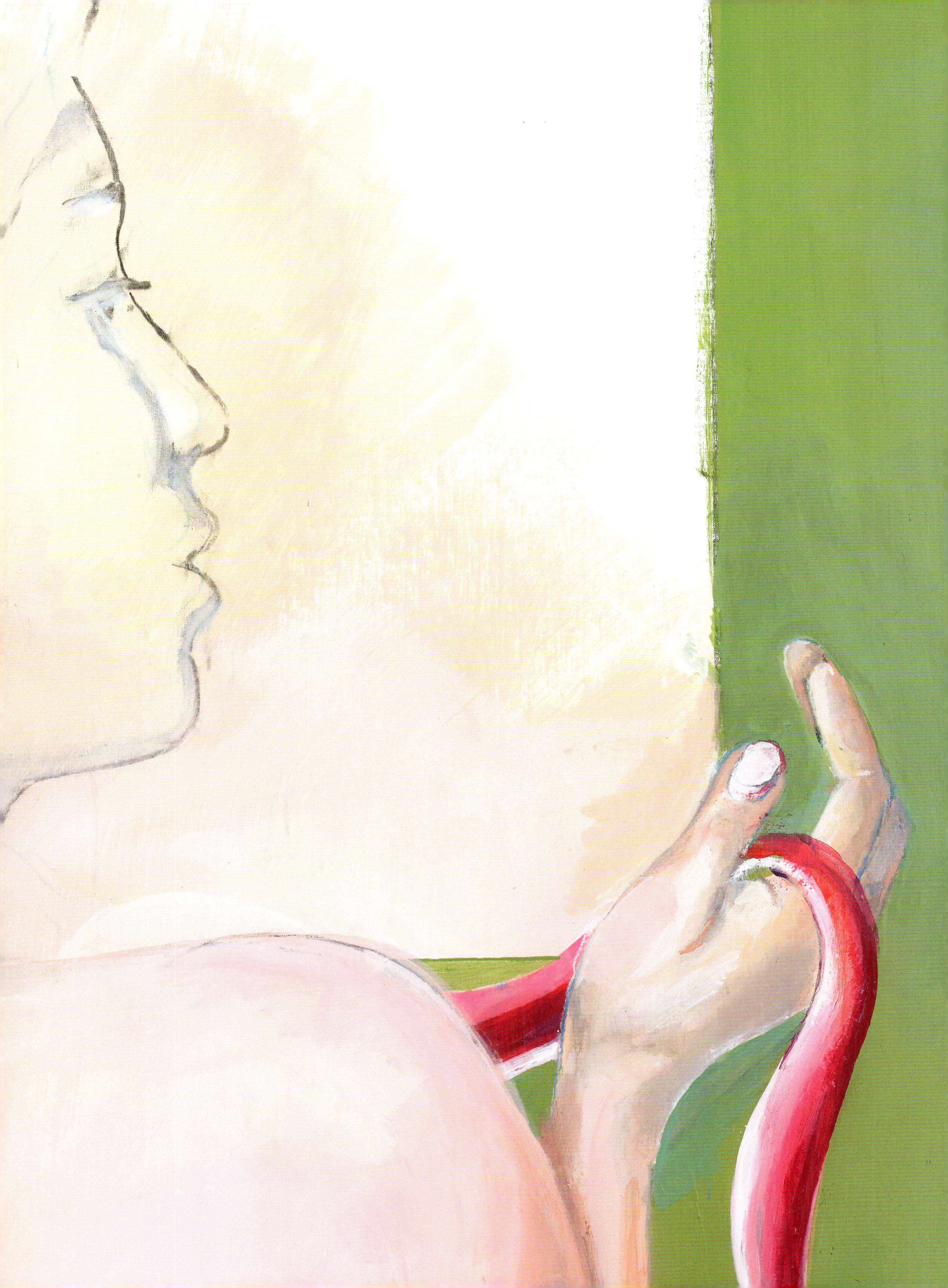

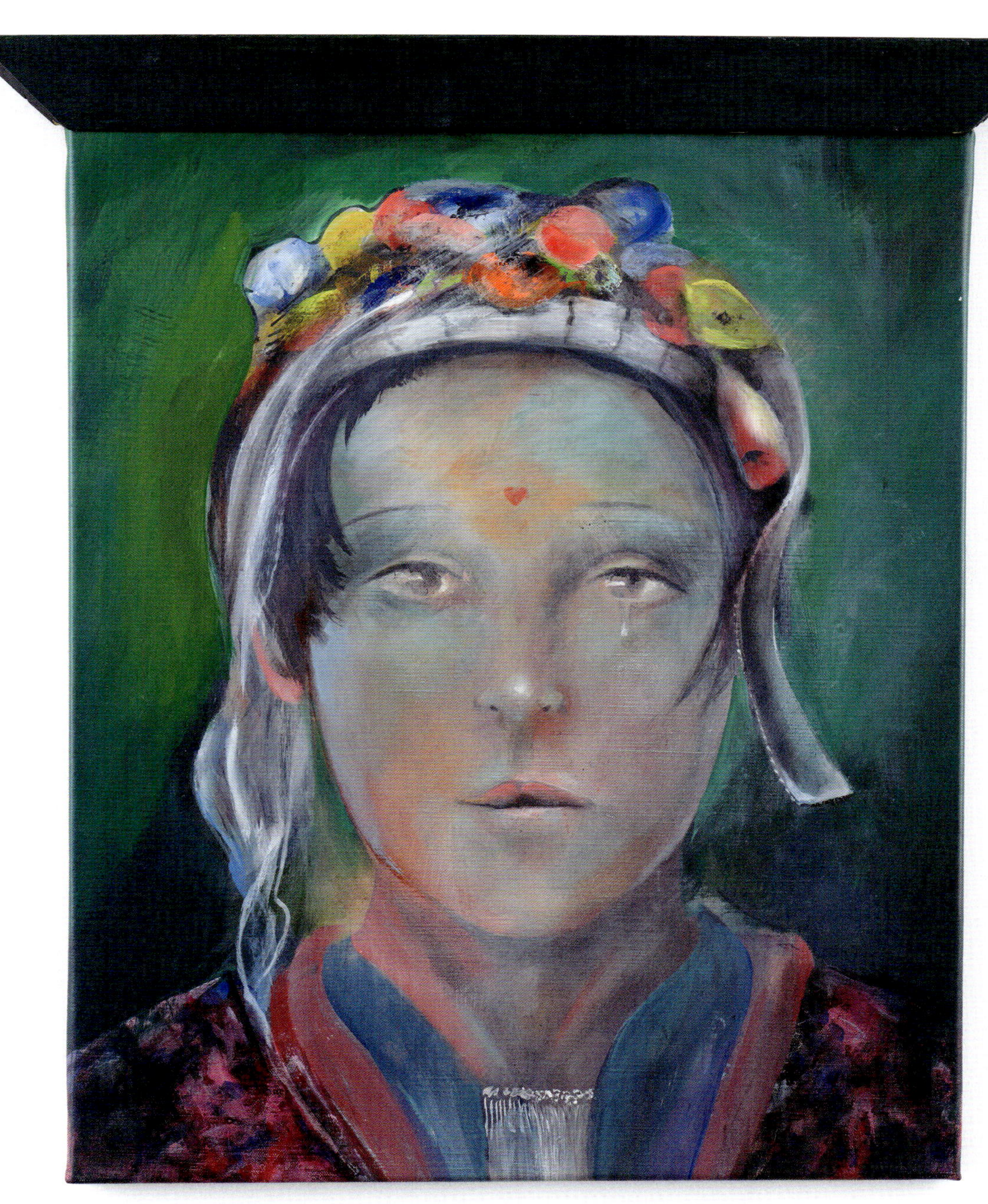

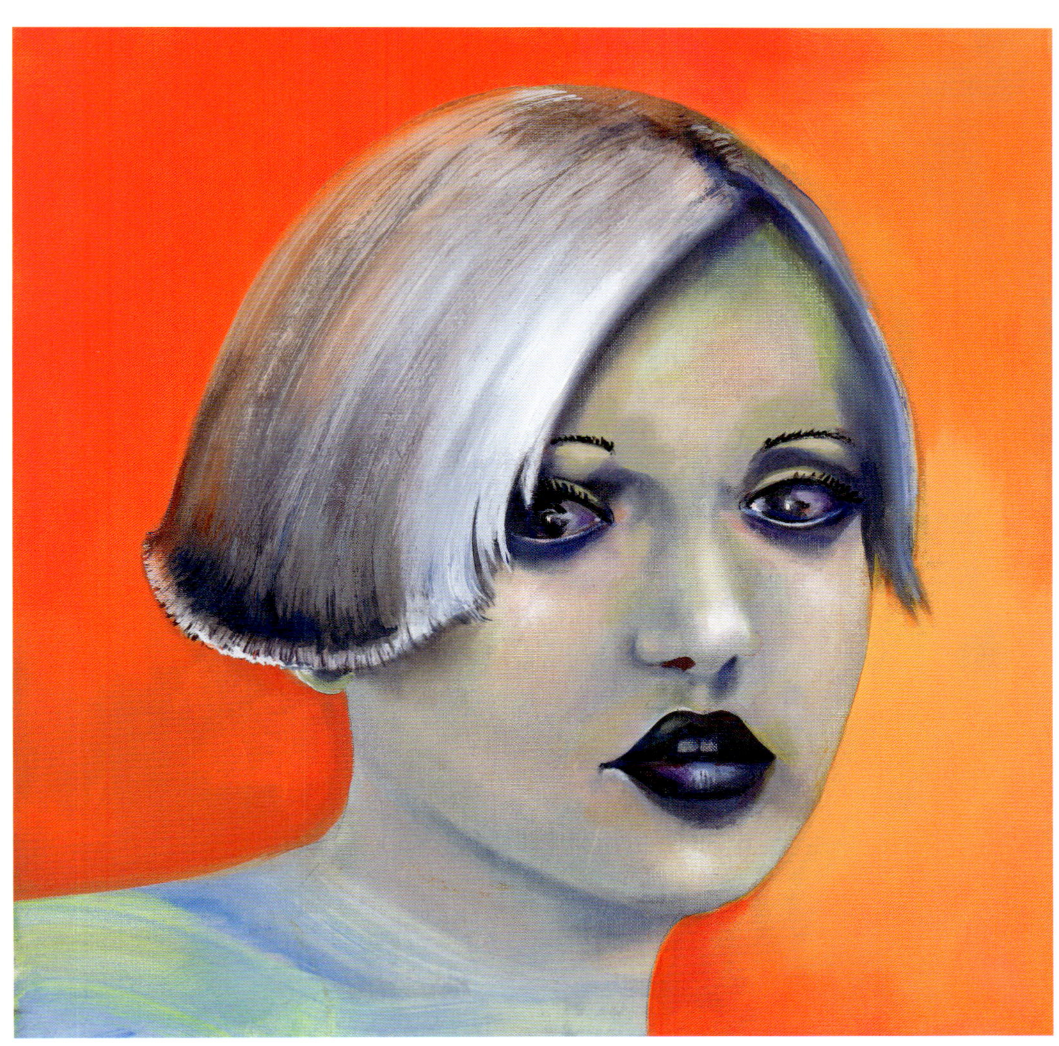

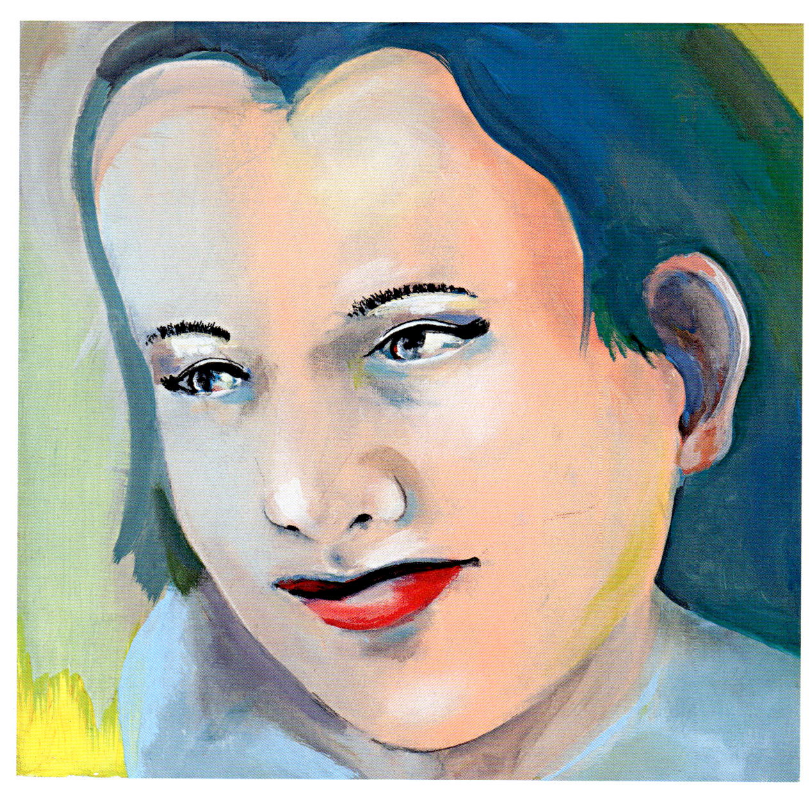

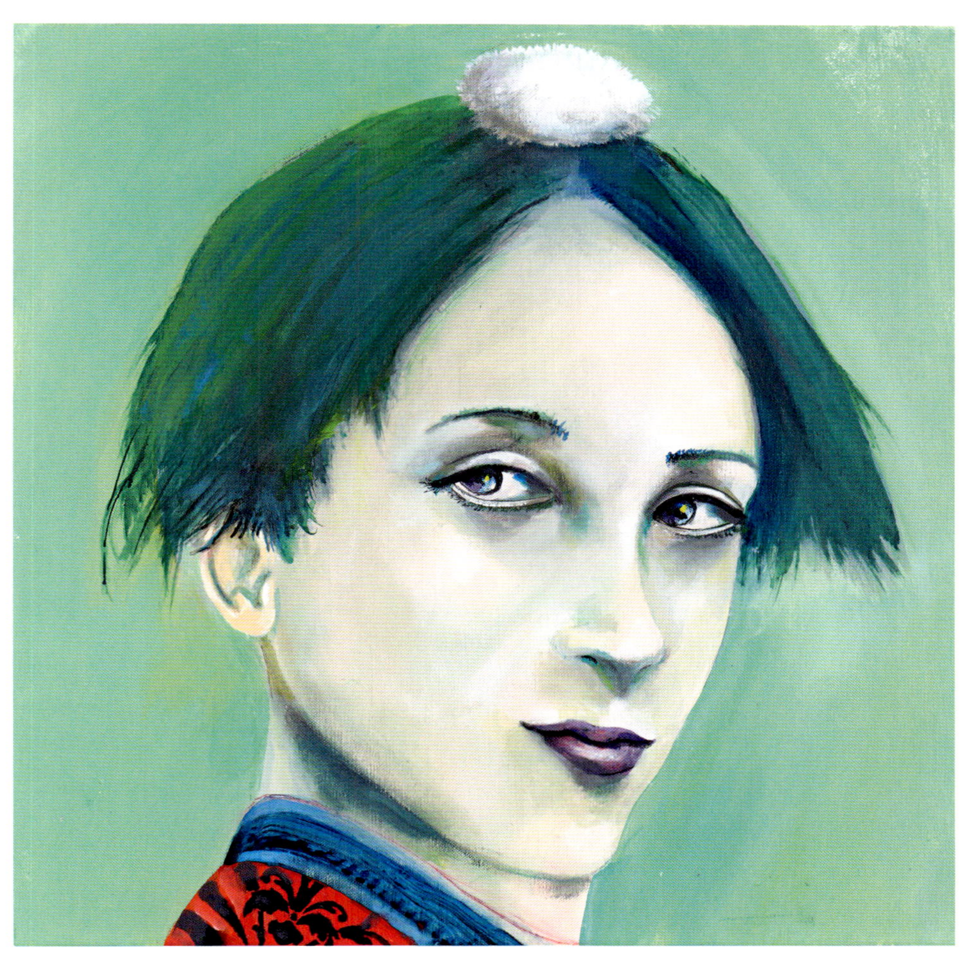

ANTONINA LEI VA BALLARE QUESTA SERA 2017

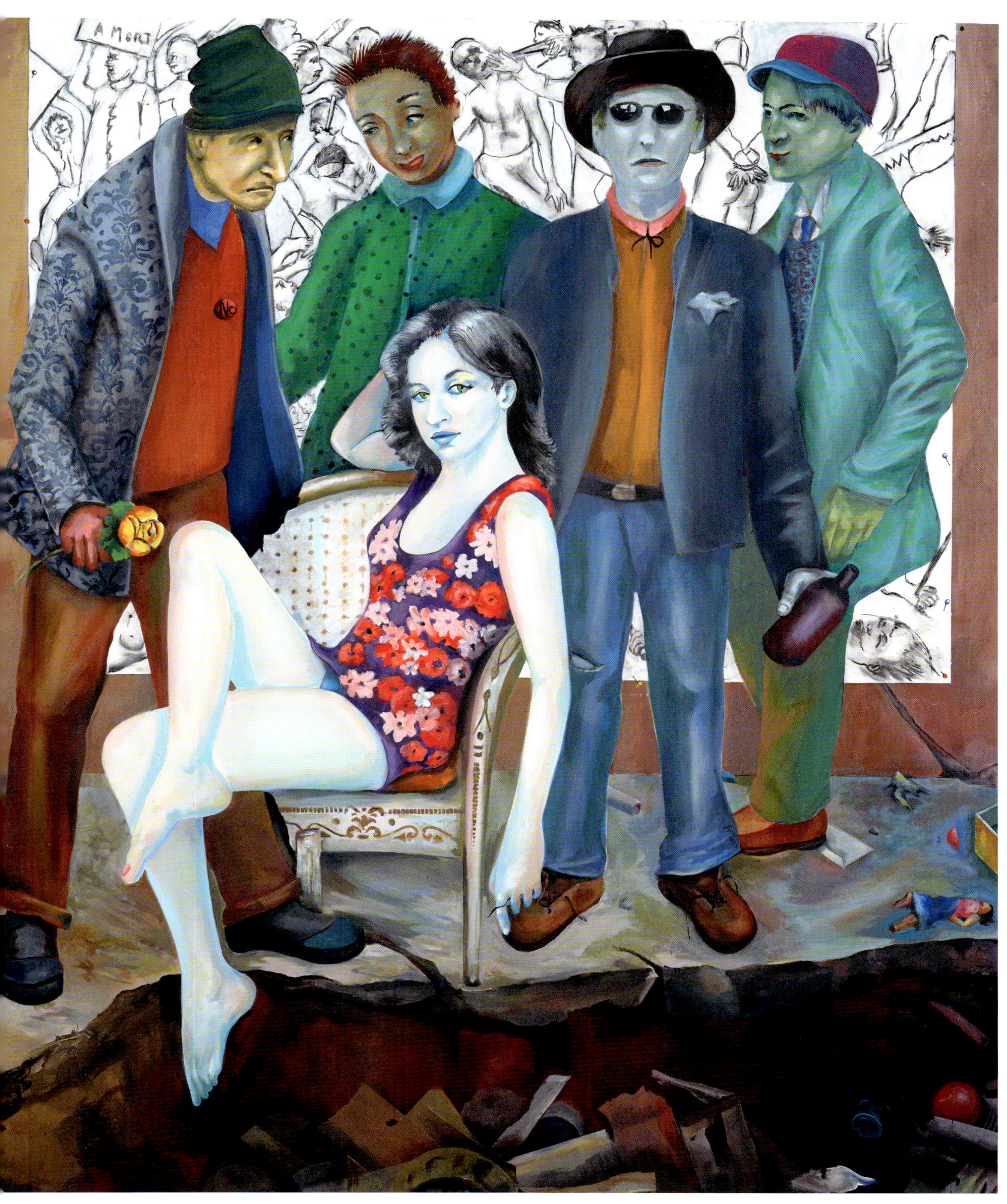
A MORT
No

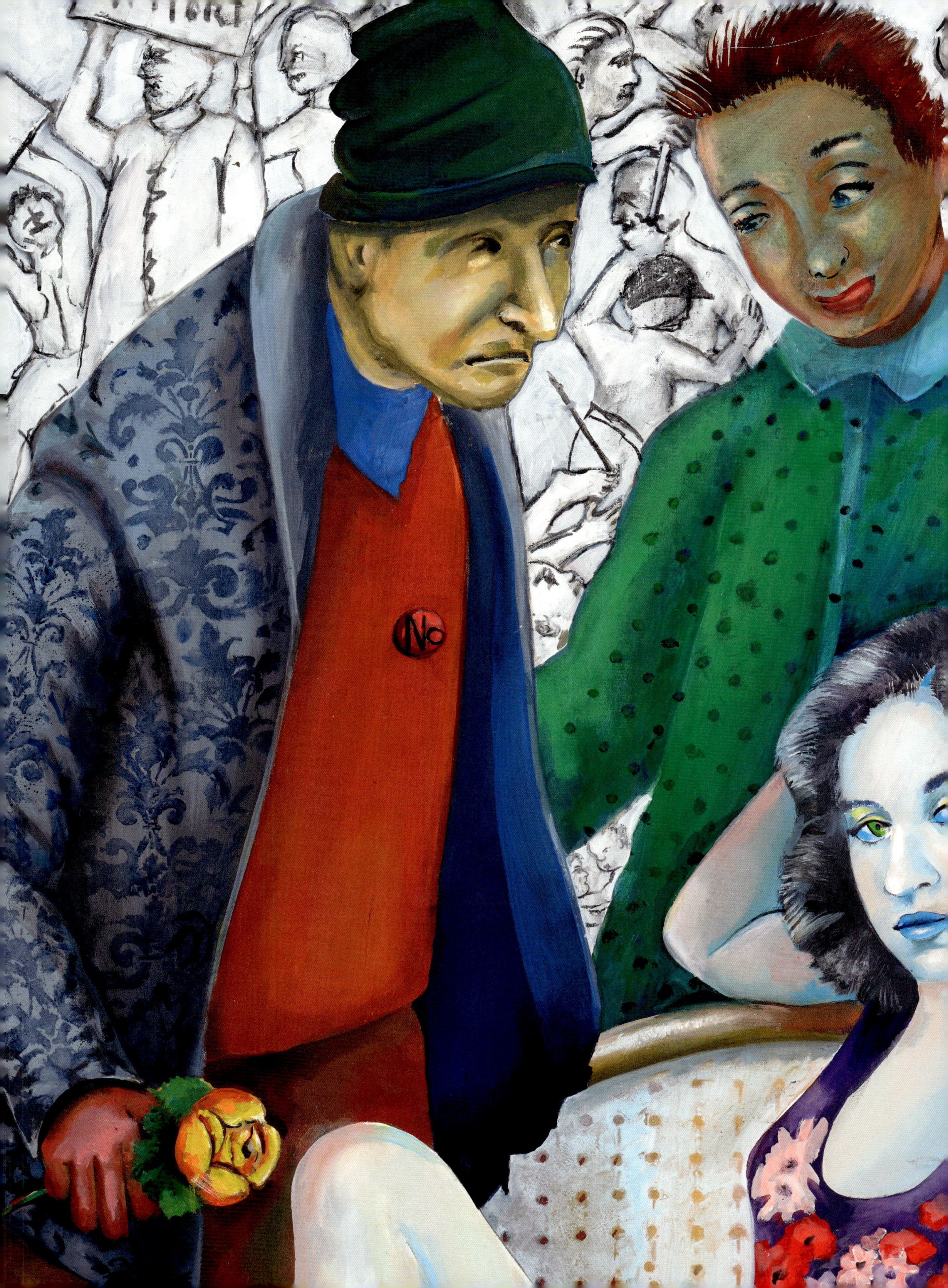
No

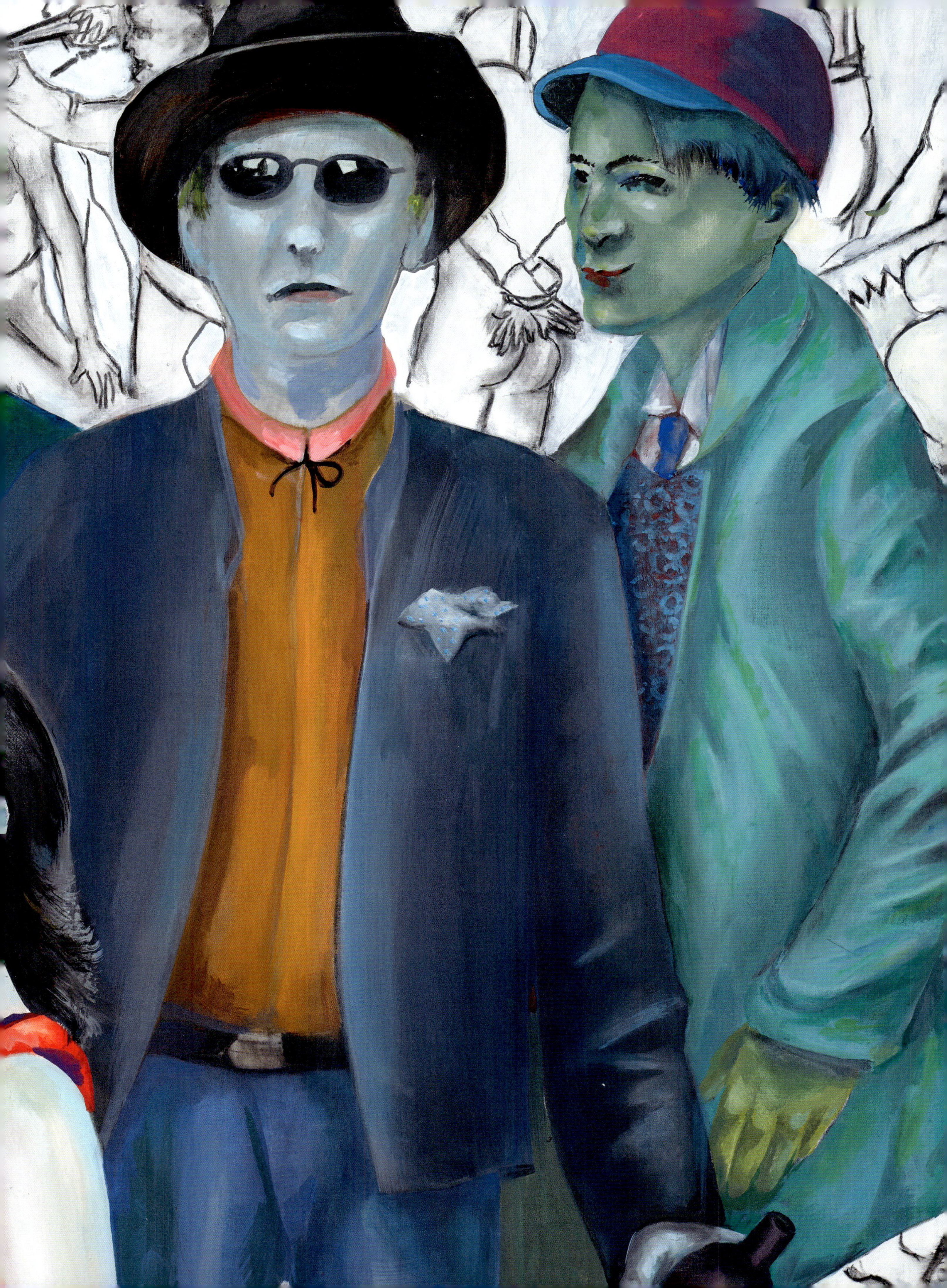

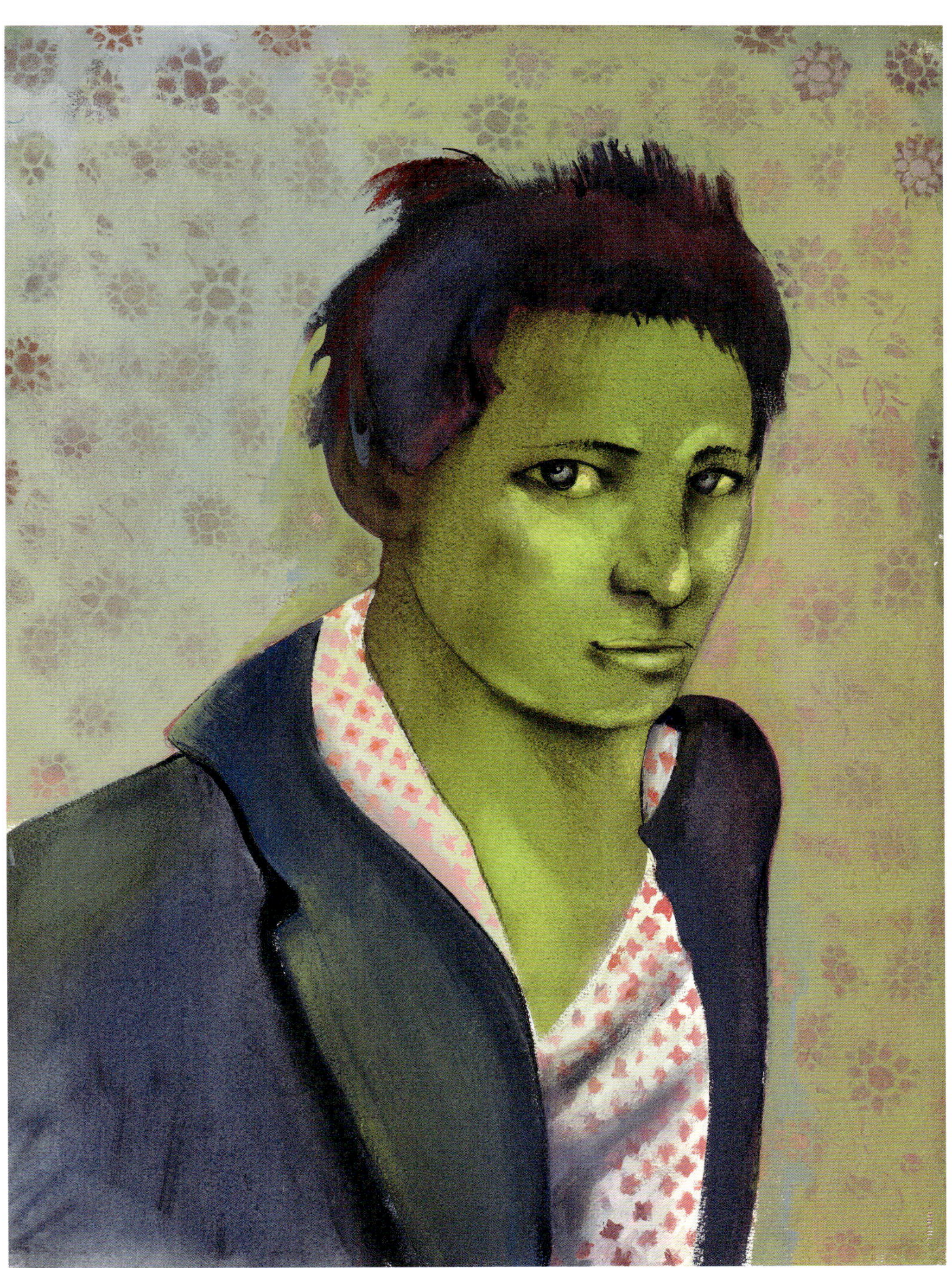

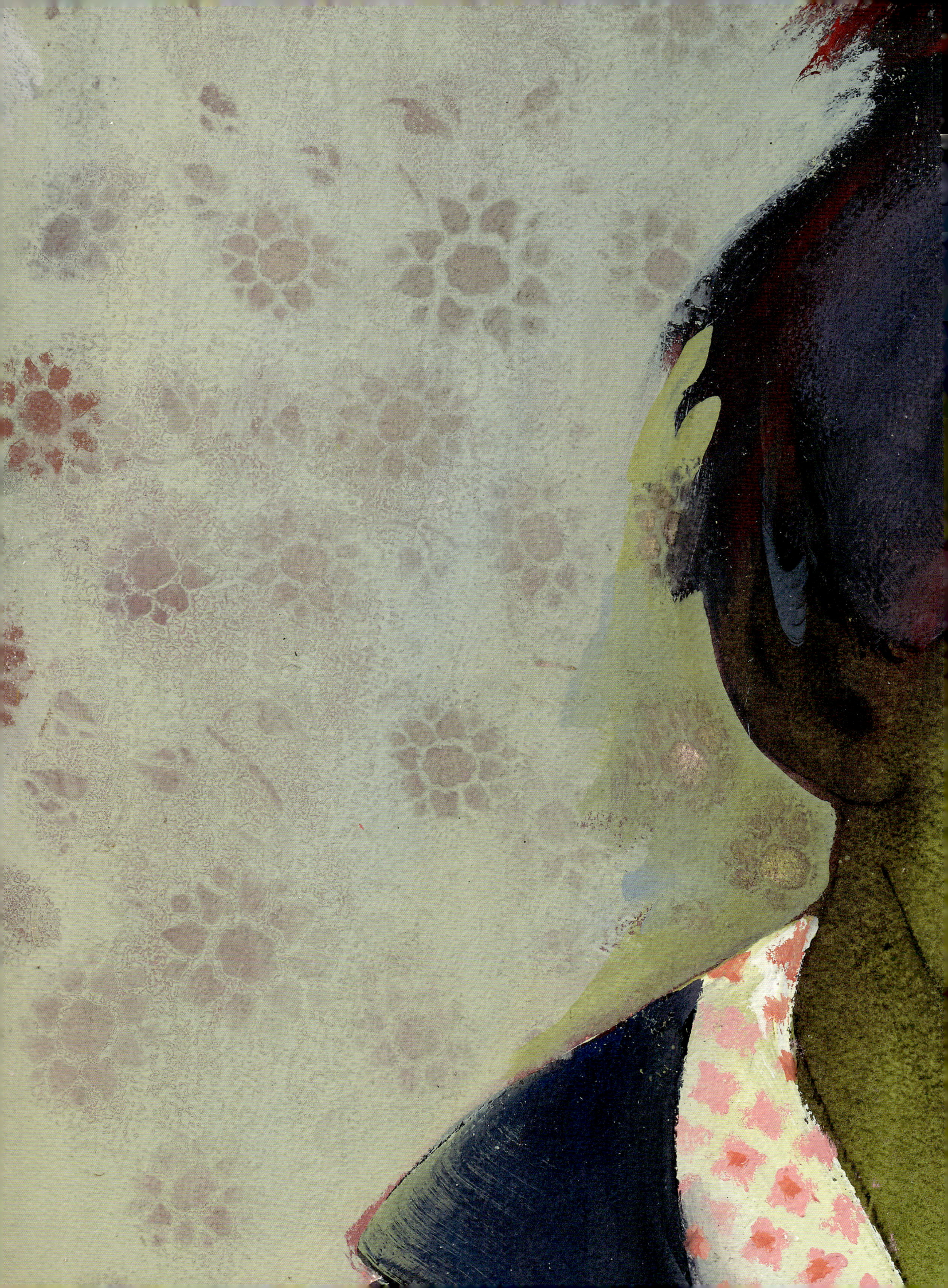

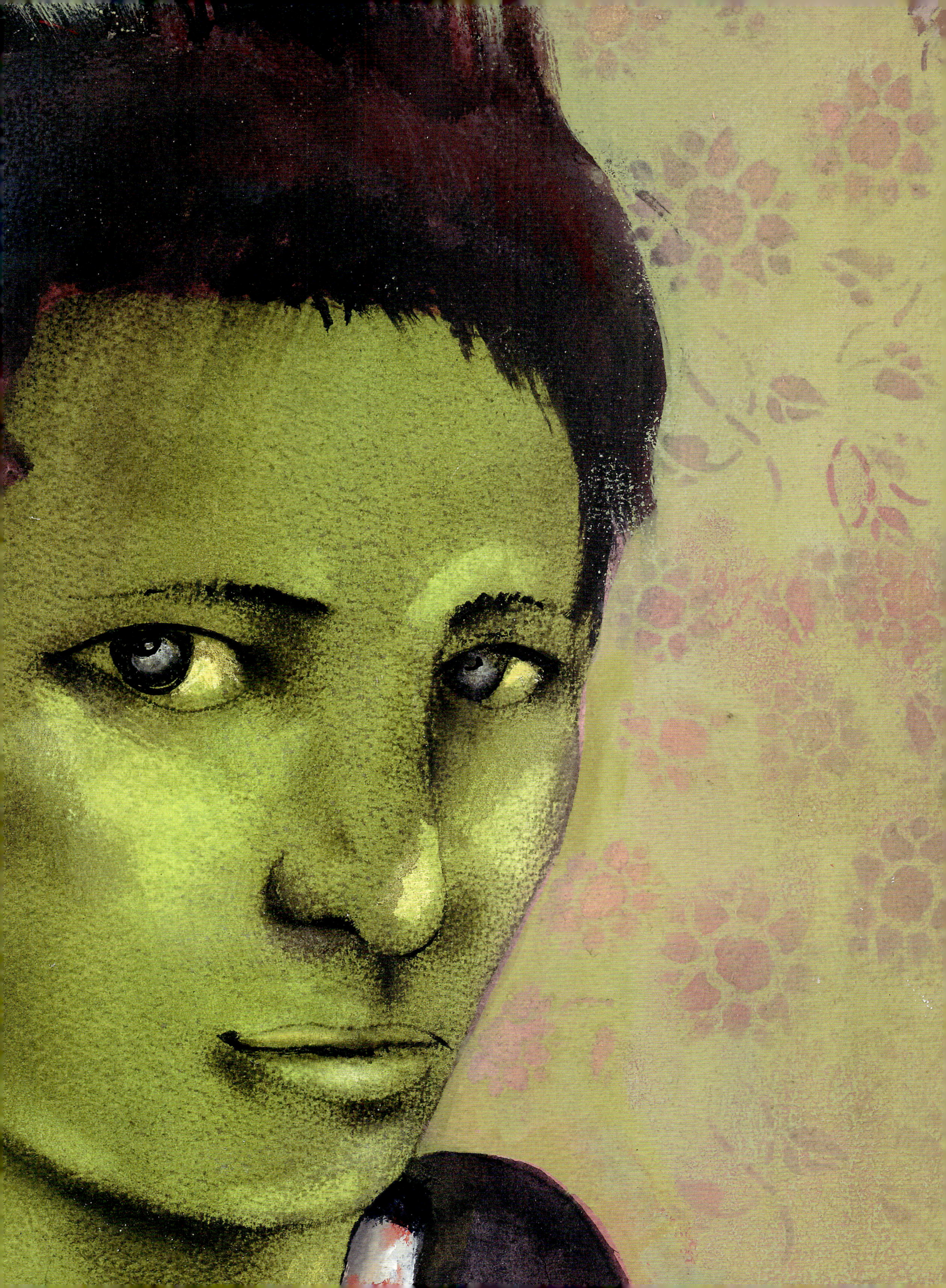

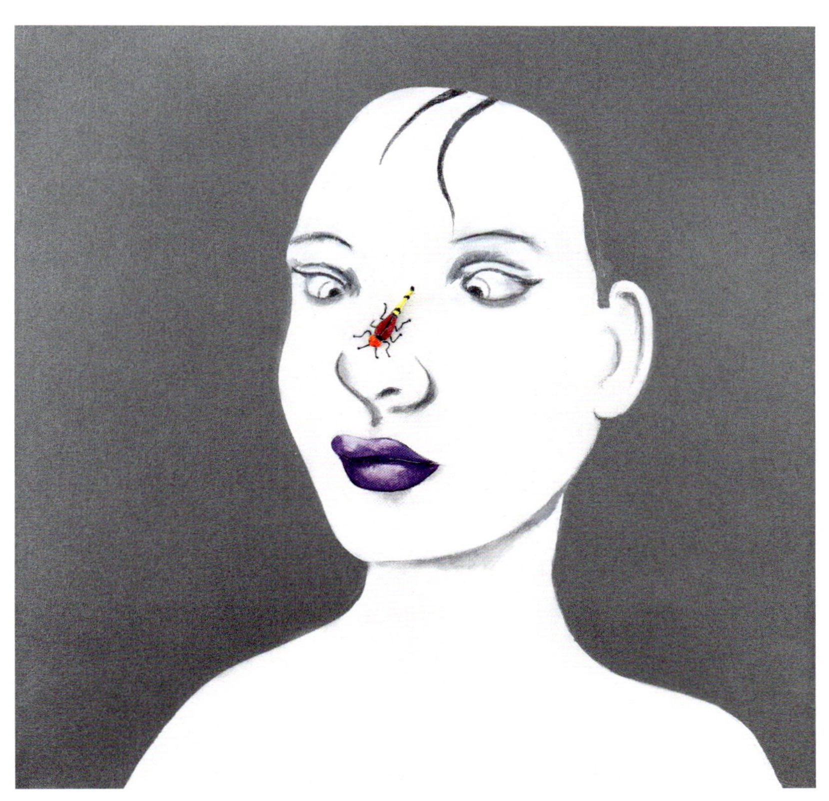

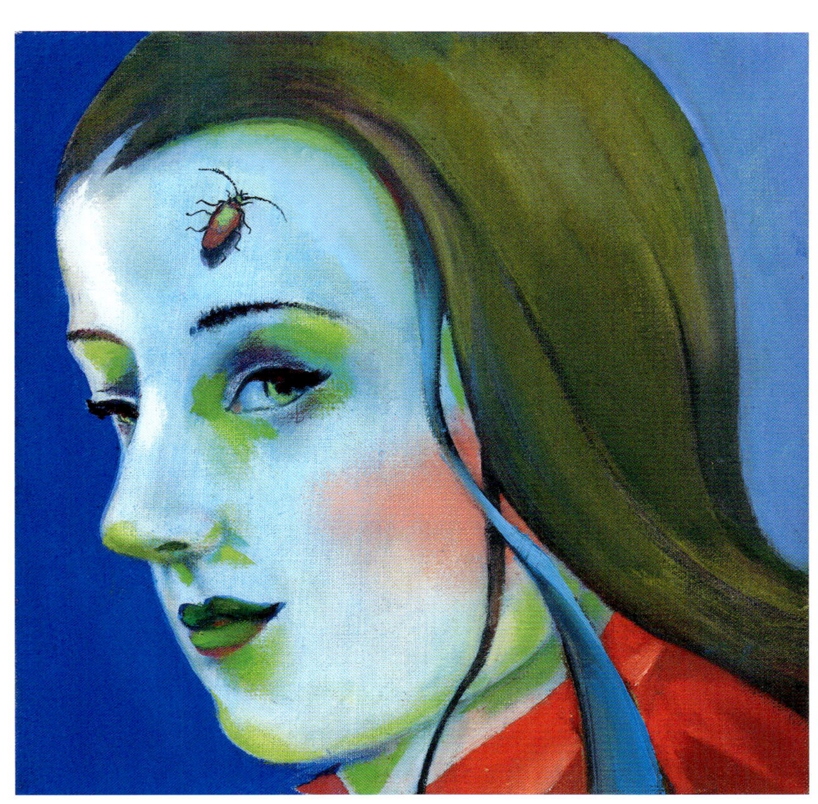

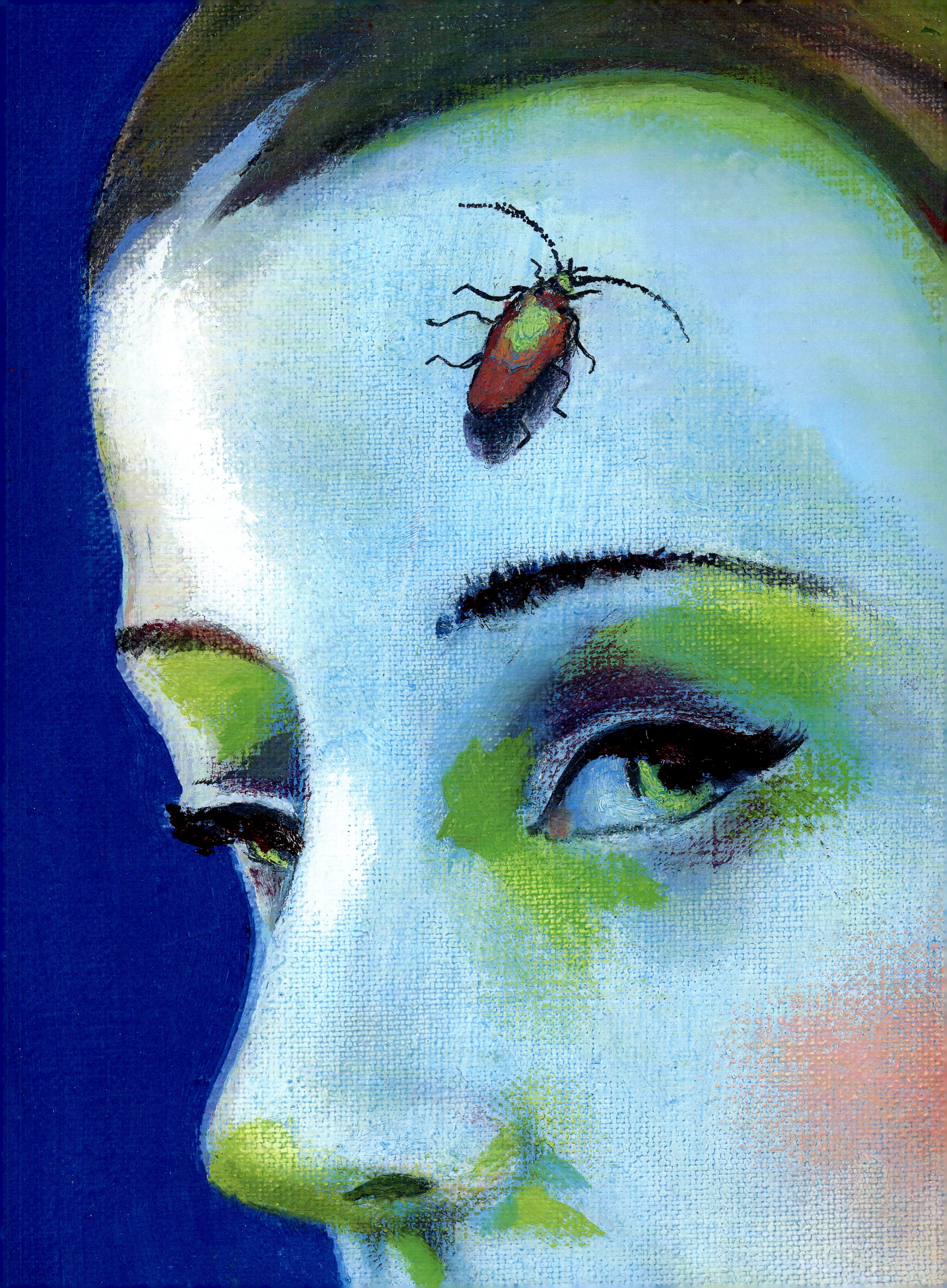

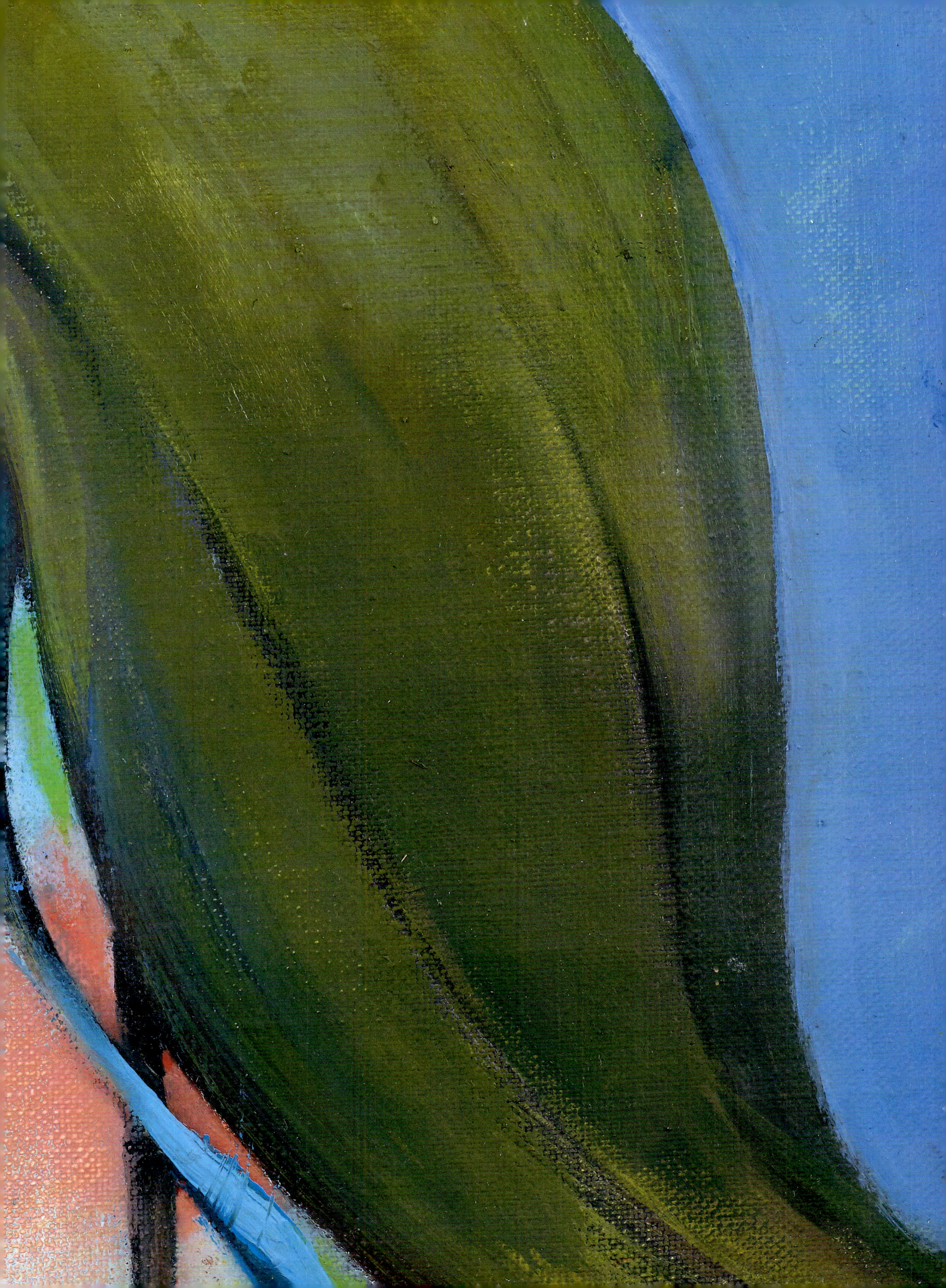

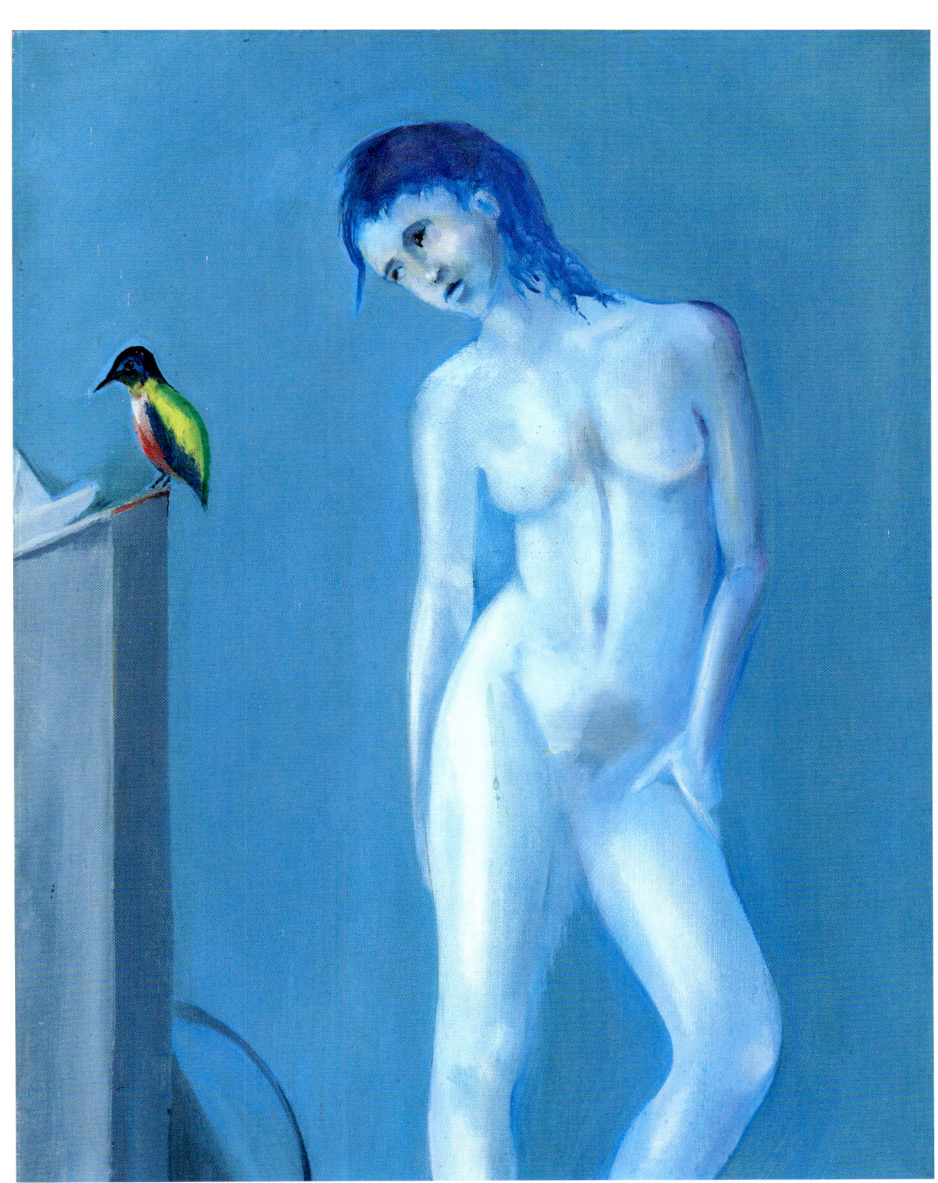

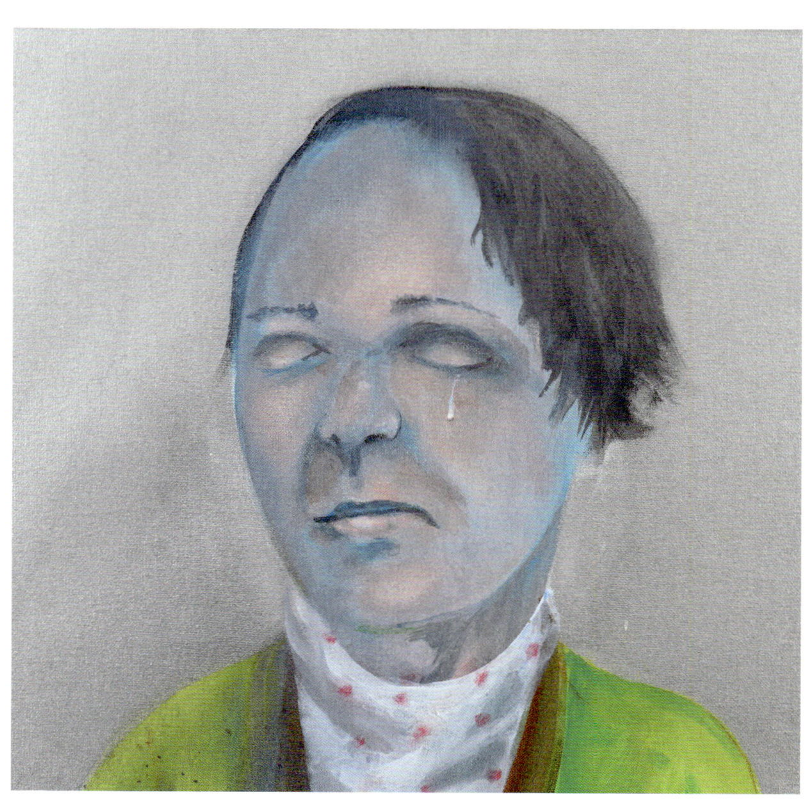

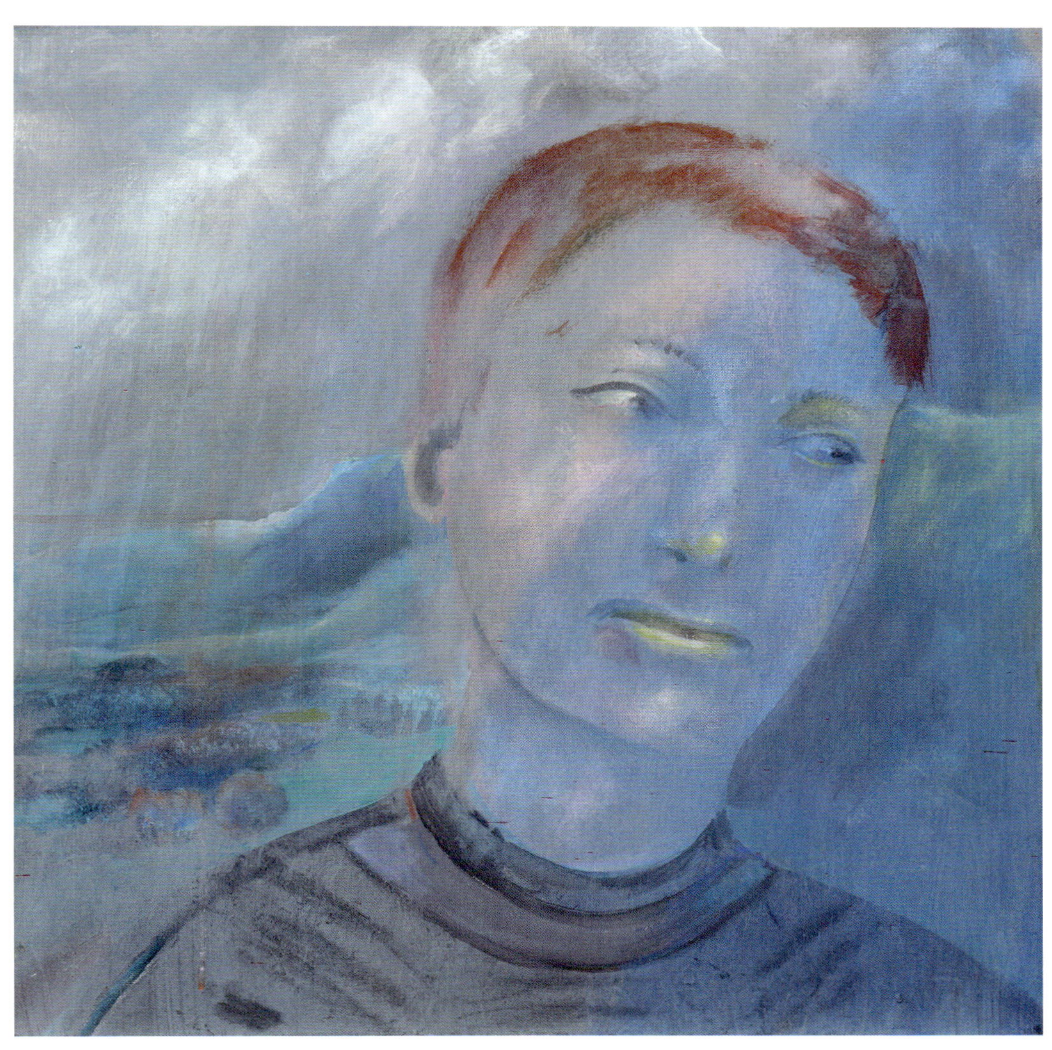

IL VAUT MIEUX NE PAS Y PENSER LAURENT 2017

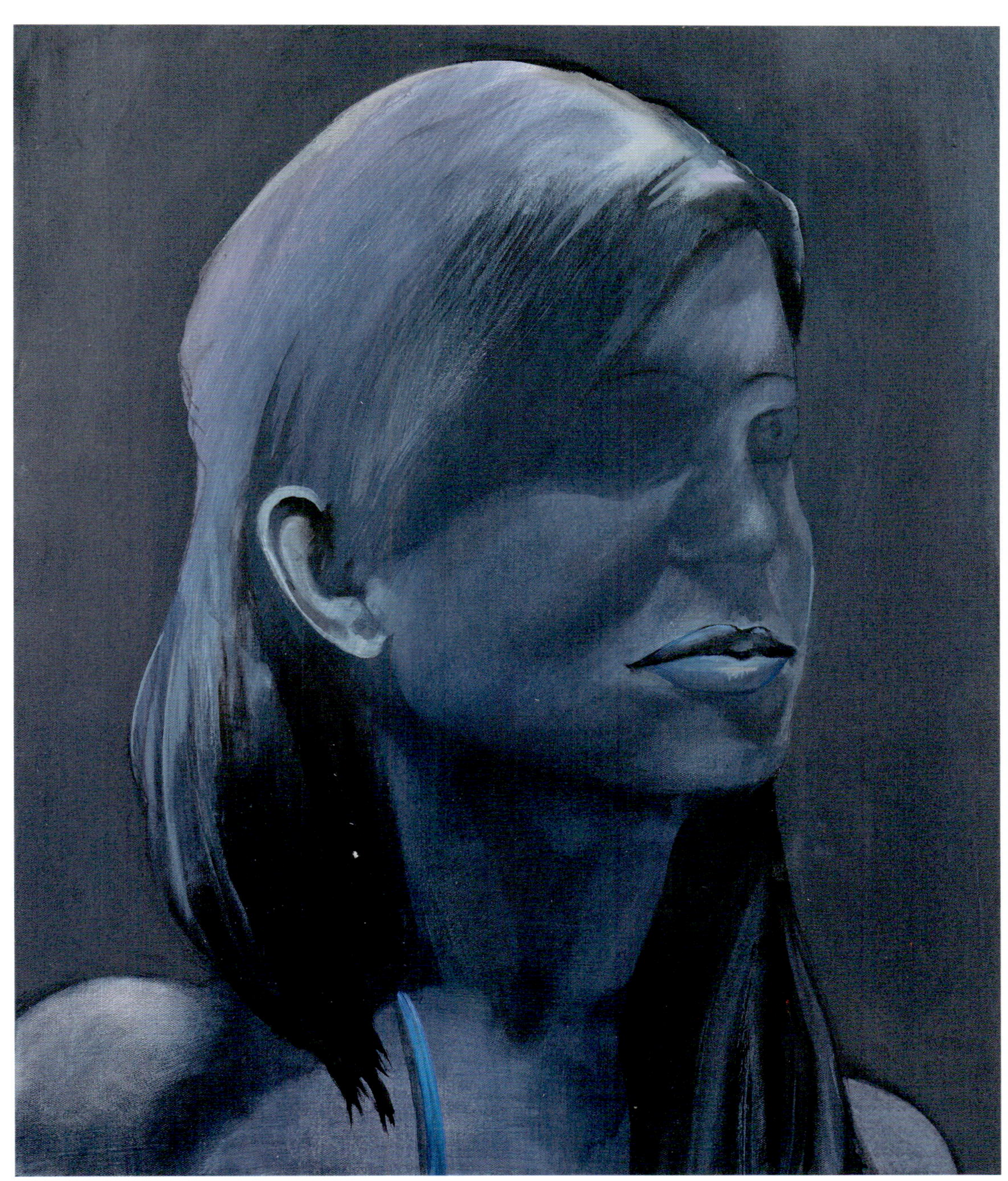

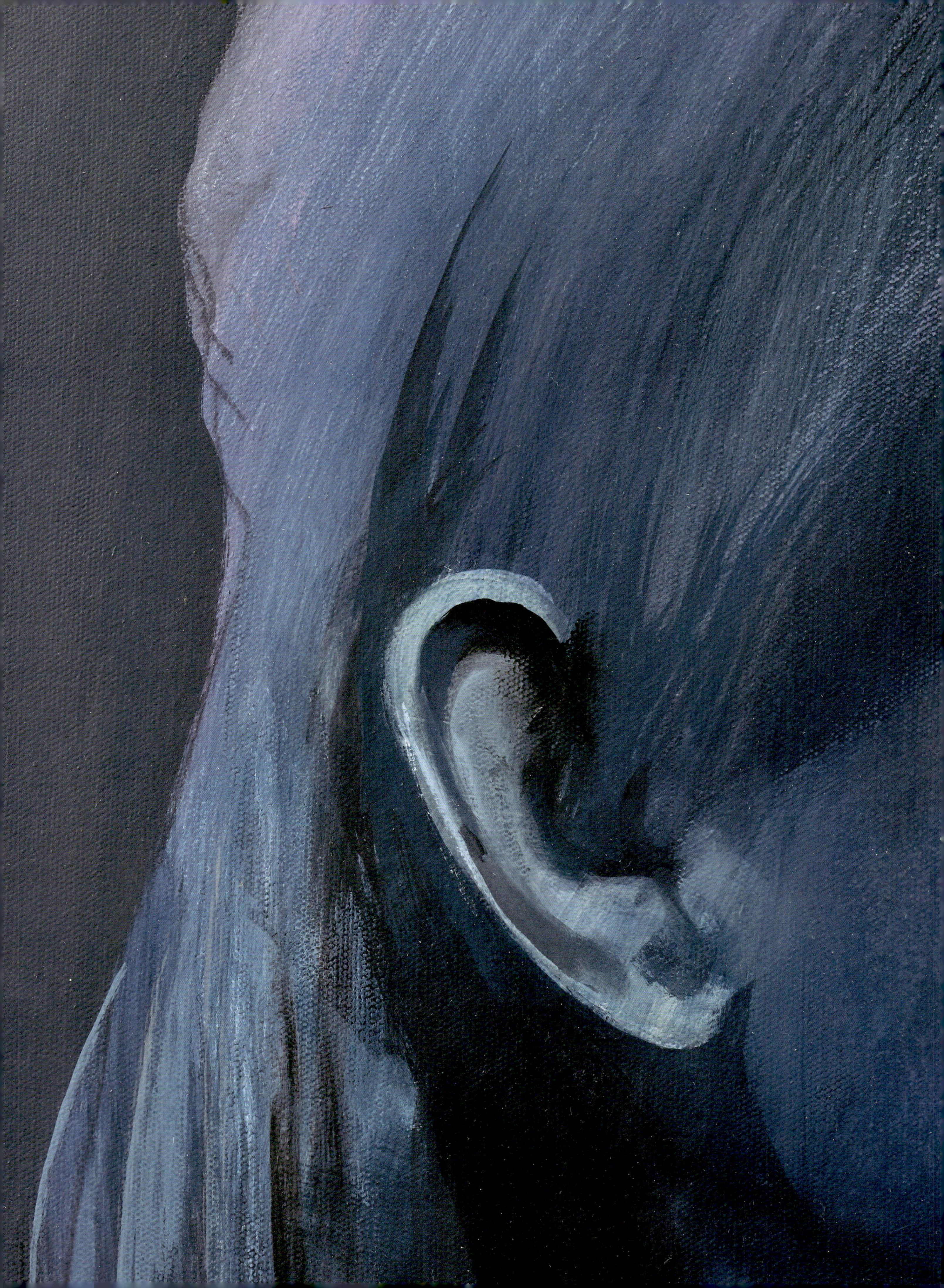

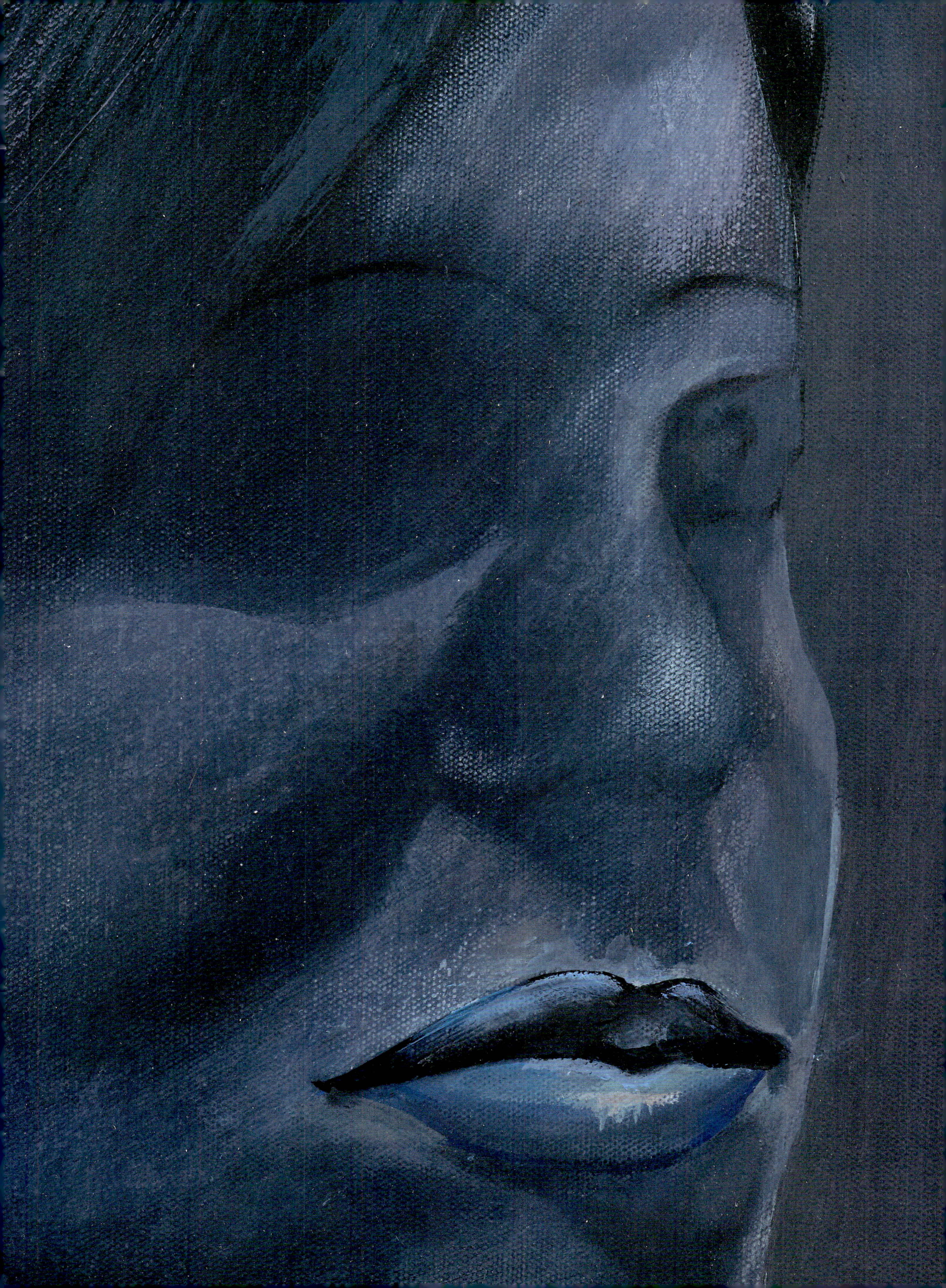

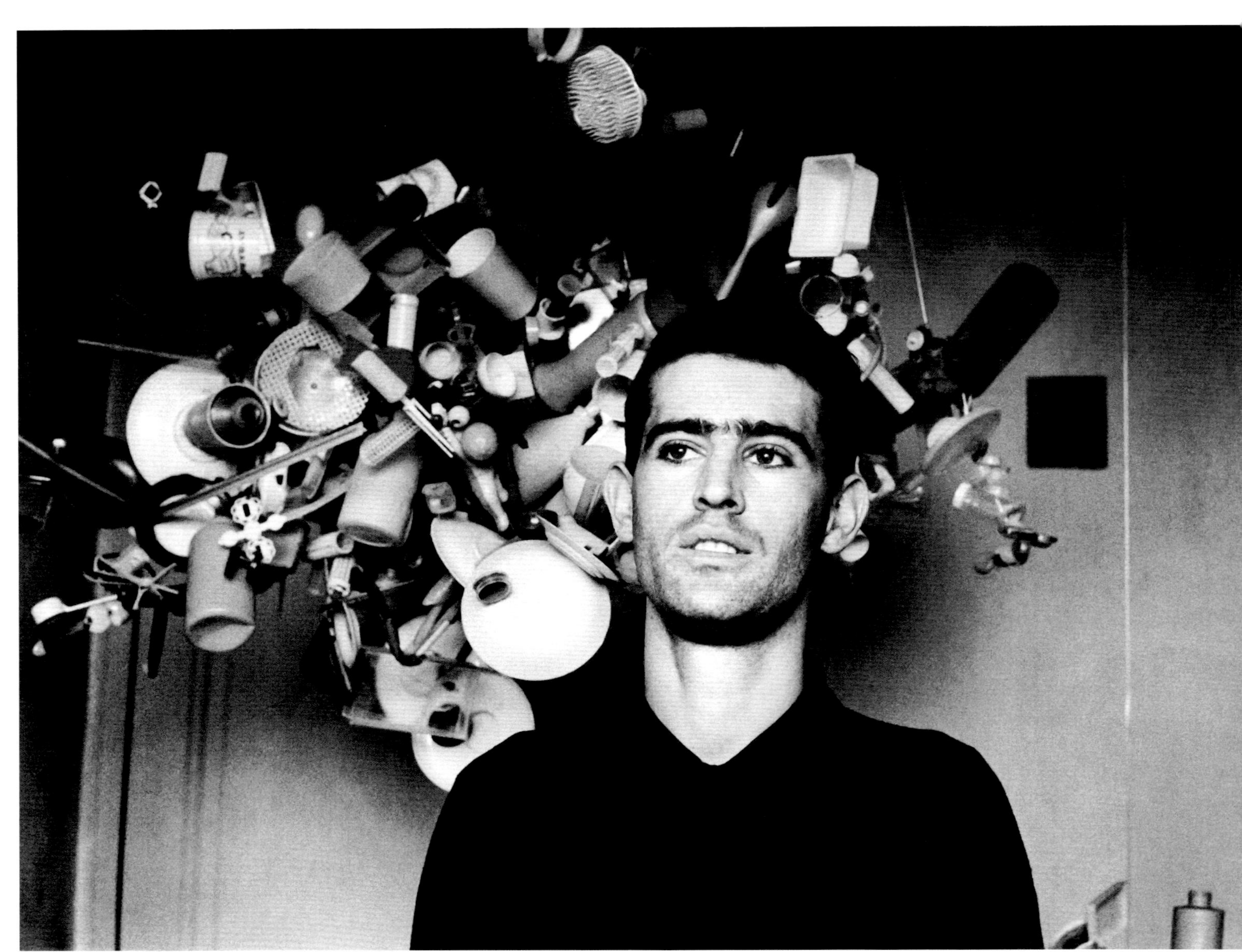

Martial Raysse in front of an early assemblage, c. 1962

I have a thousand things to put in order

I have a thousand things to put in order before I go to bed tonight.

During this flight from Copenhagen what a pleasure it was imagining Ingres looking at the first photograph.

Couldn't Impressionism be thought of as an attraction for photography...does one say for or towards... attraction towards...

It rains continually in this land of lemon-drop half-colors as the intermission finishes off Paris, that beautiful, dumb ass.

Impressionism...both the attraction for photography in its desire to capture the fleeting moment and also a last ditch defense of the act of painting using the personal touch...the "handmade" touch...with the awkwardness and imprecision which that implies in opposition to the mechanical quality of the "photographic rendering".

The "Don't move, please!" against the shimmering air.

That was a battle that had its partisans.

(I'm extremely fond of suspension points.)

Since technique thus becomes the painter's justification, ultimate and unavowed, this naturally leads through a certain aspect of abstract art, to confusing ends and means...that is to say that the impressionistic touch which was only one part of a whole has become a subject in itself and has swollen to fill the entire picture.

Cubism, in an attempt to be true...true in the manner a photograph is true...came along pasting bits of reality into collage. Next, in order to diversify style, analogous elements were introduced, manner became matter, and slipping from one analogy to another, from one period to another, tenderly were studied, first, spots on the pavement, splotches on asphalt streets, then crumbling walls and shredded posters. Substitutes replaced actual creation...a step that many took with praiseworthy simplicity.

We can allow ourselves enough naiveness to repeat that the important thing is not to be able to use an electronic device to reproduce a Kandinsky but to discover a new way to structure surfaces...to repeat that technique is nothing...that only the results are important.

Five years ago, as I was getting out of a bus, it occurred to me that it wasn't the use of new techniques and materials that made a work novel but rather the search for new surface construction.

I wanted my works to possess the serene self-evidence of mass-produced refrigerators...to have the look of new, sterile, inalterable visual hygiene. Life is horrible. It's evident we are going to die. Thus we become even closer accomplices of all that bears within itself the seed of death...to use this as a means of arousing emotion is what I term speculation on cellular decay. During this period everyone was working with an abstract expressionistic stroke on objects or with objects and the art galleries looked like the "flea market." Today you would look in vain for the slightest trace of life there. The galleries have become huge clinics for white and bloodless pictures...all I dreamed of. As for painting, it's gone elsewhere. The only advantage the artist has over the machine or over the numerous domains on the fringe of art that use the machine, is that the artist, at any rate, always does things a whole lot worse...the inversion of poles, subversion, even, in his realm. This idea corresponded to the liking I felt for the work of bad painters. Awkwardness moves us because it overrides the rules in its search for true feeling. To track life down in the realm of color, I tried using plastics, fluorescence, relationships that were untrue, out of key, or paintings with errors… flawed and faulty…or bad taste…the hideous and the horrible. And now, especially, by using neon and artificial lighting, I seek in transcendental color a substitute for life. Neon also favors movement that is without agitation. It gives the idea of action or of spring bottled-up.

As Penelope approaches and touches Ulysses

he undoes her tunic ceremoniously

beneath

she's in

an (Olympic)

swimming suit

Since Pop art, like every other form of art, results when the individuals involved reflect upon their personal culture, Pop art is profoundly affected by an unavowed attraction for the style of the 30s.

That is why it is closer to Mae West than to Cape Kennedy.

Painting is not an obstacle race. Works of art and careers cannot be judged by the sort of monthly appraisals that are becoming a habit with us. It's only now that we can look objectively at the nonfigurative period and distinguish the true creators from the followers; yet even so, it is impossible to determine the exact distance that separates them from Picasso, for example.

The unconditioned eye does not exist. The general public sees the world today with eyes that were developed by the Impressionist painters…this education of perception being spread by means of newspapers, publicity and so forth. A painter exerts an action upon perception, engineers vision, but what was I going to say? Oh yes… vision, a psychological phenomenon, subjective…and emotional… In a room where a definite color determines the prevailing tone, the beloved will change color in relation to her surroundings. If you look at a face and fix your attention on the nose, the nose will not only change its size but also its color in relation to the rest of the face. These were the observations that I wanted to translate in the works I termed "a geometrie variable" (variable geometry). For example, in the big painting entitled "Paysage à géométrie variable et à Martial Raysse kilomètres-heure" exhibited at Venice, each element was treated as a world in itself, with its own particular color scheme and scale, independently of the others, in order to express the attention that was directed to this specific part of the landscape at a given moment. All of those elements, taken together, constituted a picture which was a seismographic record of the psychological variations of the painting act considered as a life act. The special shape chosen permitted me to define a basic space that would convey my ideas the most conveniently. This choice is based on the following considerations and coming from the field of "l'art d'assemblage" where the objects I utilized were common property. I had for a long time felt the need of creating prefabricated objects of my own, my prototypes…to replace the stereotypes of society with my own personal ones… It was in this sense that I defined a certain shape of mouth and eye, or certain elements like palm trees, chickens, boats, etc., which I could use in a given context to express certain personal psychological definitions.

I wish to emphasize that my works do not employ variable elements but variable geometry. This distinction is fundamental, for these elements are not parts of a game that can be shifted within the framework of the specific in picture surface that has been defined once and for all. Not at all, for if this were true it would merely represent another form of action painting with an abstract expressionistic structuration. For me it is the very geometry of the work itself that is variable, which is to say, it is the space determined by its boundaries and the psychological comparisons that result determined by the proximity or the separation of these elements. This form seems to me much like our own existence where all the elements are profoundly dissimilar, but where they are brought into co-existence by an act of will that coincides with the very notion of life itself.

Like a mass-produced refrigerator
like the knees of the lady opposite you
in the subway
Beautiful
Beautiful as what
Making a picture

In 1945, painting was running two worlds behind schedule. Abstract Expressionism, which should have taken place almost immediately after the initial experiences of Kandinsky, became a language of gesticulation at the end of World War II that was a completely natural one for war veterans.

And so it goes.

The so-called painting of the present is nothing but a layer of fossils peacefully building up a transition stage that has no connection with the life we are living....

And for that matter, our life is elsewhere...not in the antiquated lodgings and logic that are ours...for Park Avenue and the freshly scraped Arc de Triomphe are both just as out of date.

Painting begins tomorrow. It will be the work of young artists that are to come.

MARTIAL RAYSSE

Originally published in *Martial Raysse*, the catalogue that accompanied the exhibition of the same name, presented in 1967 by Dwan Gallery, Los Angeles.

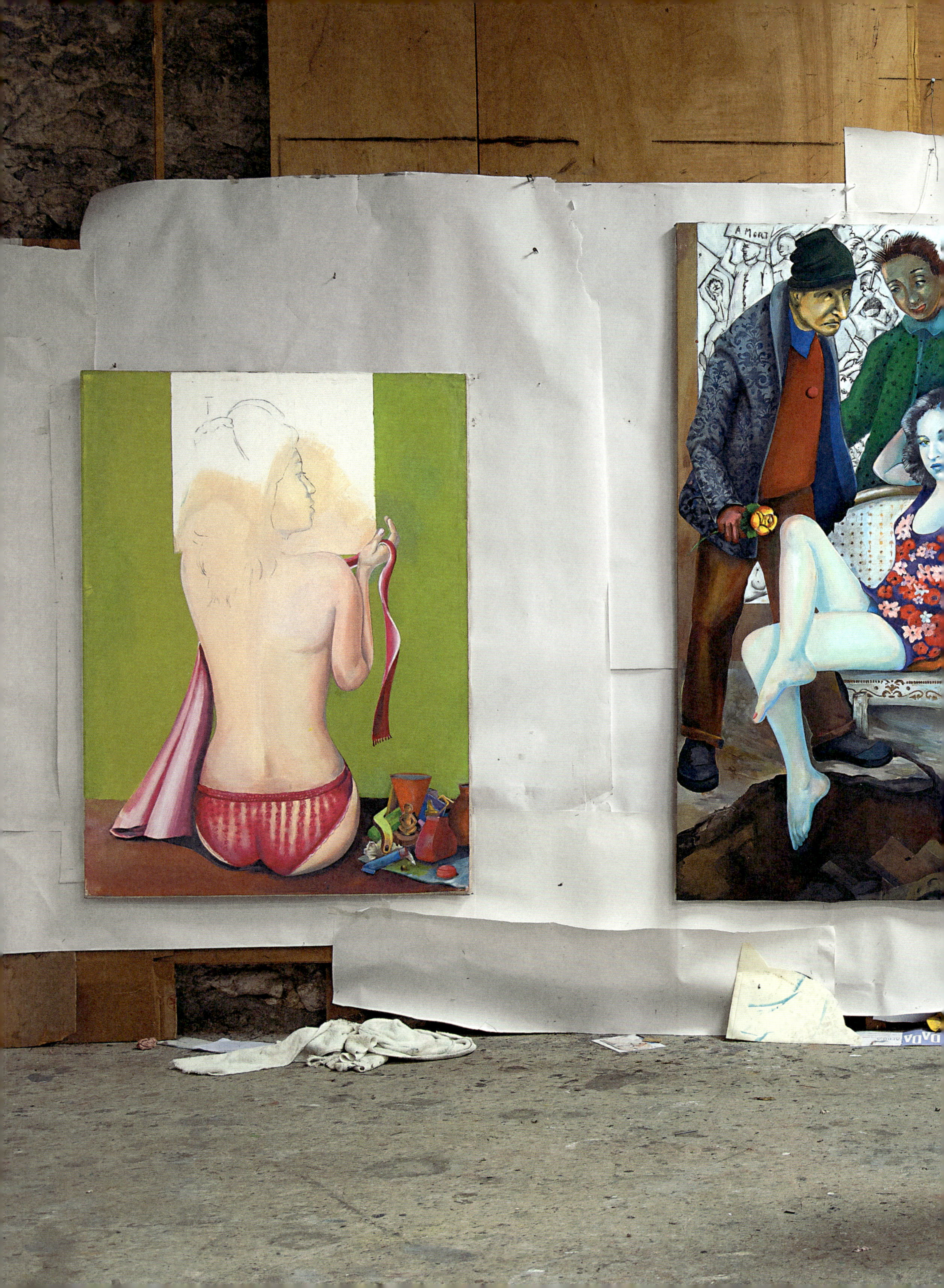
A MORT
DADA

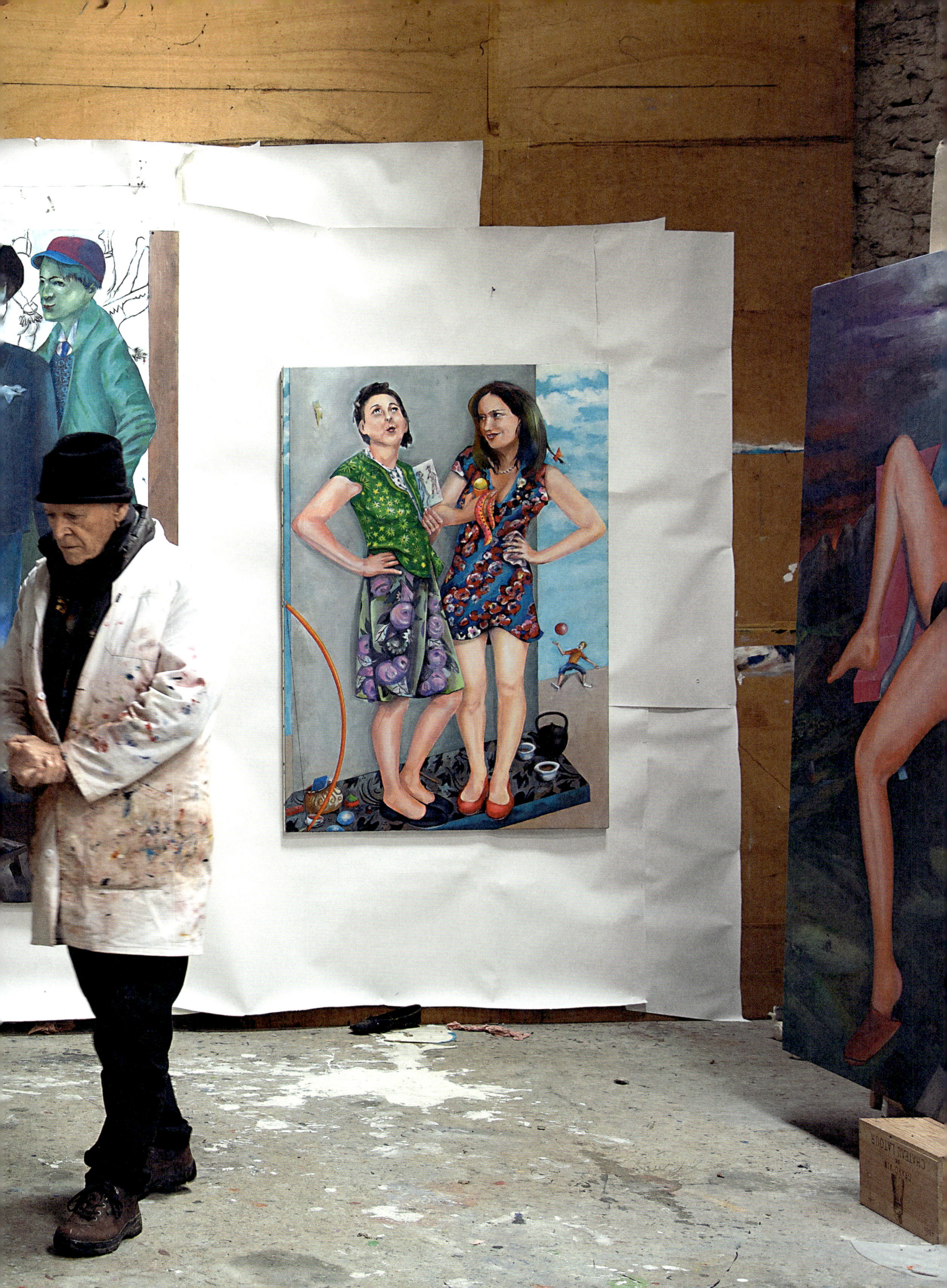
GRAND VIN
DE
CHATEAU LATOUR

Selected Chronology

The following timeline is adapted from the chronology compiled by Mica Gherghescu and published in* Martial Raysse*, the exhibition catalogue for the artist's 2014 retrospective at the Centre national d'art et de culture Georges Pompidou. That document is based on the biography written by Véronique Dabin for Raysse's 1993 retrospective at the Galerie nationale du Jeu de Paume.

1936–1940s

Martial Raysse is born on February 12, 1936 into a family of ceramicists in Golfe-Juan, Vallauris, on the French Riviera near Nice. He is profoundly affected by his parents' participation in the French Resistance during World War II and will later recall: "I know what it's like to be pulled out of bed at three in the morning by the Gestapo."[1]

At age 12, he first experiments with poetry and visual art, and remembers, "I started to draw and paint very spontaneously, after seeing quite a lot of bad paintings. At the age of twelve I was doing my first watercolors…At sixteen, hiding from my parents, I was painting in the cellar by the light of a candle. I was working at the time with a trowel. I made a sort of matter painting out of white plaster."[2]

1954

Raysse studies literature at the University of Nice and attends the Ecole Nationale des Arts décoratifs de Nice, run by François Bret, co-founder of the *Peintres de vingt ans* group.

1955

Though initially intending to pursue writing, after reflecting on the limitations of language Raysse decides to become a painter. Throughout his career, painting and writing are intrinsically linked in his work, especially in his poem/objects.

Raysse meets artists Ben Vautier (also known as Ben) and Arman at the *Club des jeunes*, an informal salon held in the basement of a *brasserie* in Nice. Led by art critic Jacques Lepage, the energetic group of young artists and intellectuals convenes on Saturday afternoons to exchange ideas about art, poetry, theater, literature, and cinema.

Inspired by Jean Dubuffet's visceral impasto style, Raysse mixes sand and plaster to create textural matter paintings. He begins to make assemblages from discarded objects that he gathers from the trash and collects on the beaches of the Côte d'Azur.

1956–57

Influenced by the mobiles of Alexander Calder, Raysse makes wire sculptures that mimic movements in nature, such as wind and waves.

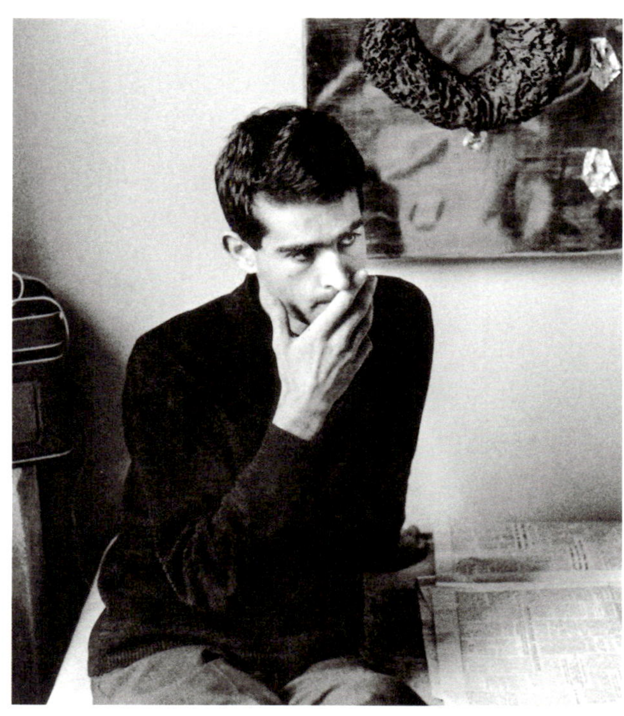

1. Martial Raysse at Yves Klein's home, Paris, c. 1960

In July 1957, Raysse shows abstract paintings at Galerie Longchamp in Nice in the group exhibition *Peintures de vingt ans*. The exhibition includes two other Nice-based artists, Claude Gilli and Albert Chubac. The following month, Raysse's work is also represented in *Mobiles,* an exhibition at Line Vautrin in Haut-de-Cagnes.

In September 1957, Raysse has a solo exhibition titled *Mobiles et peintures* at Little Galerie in Villefranche-sur-Mer.

1958

Raysse meets Yves Klein through Arman. On April 28, Klein presents *Le Vide* at Galerie Iris Clert in Paris.

Raysse's first solo exhibition at Galerie Vieil-Olivier, *Peinture-Poésie-Sculpture*, includes poem-objects, abstract paintings, and mobiles. In a letter to the artist, the poet, novelist, and playwright Jean Cocteau writes: "Your exhibition impressed me greatly in an extremely vague and treacherous area. One finds a poet there and that's very rare."[3]

In October, Ben opens a record store in Nice and holds exhibitions in the first-floor gallery, which he initially calls Laboratoire 32 and later renames Galerie Ben Doute de Tout. A site of artistic experimentation and exchange, the venue hosts a group exhibition, *Idées Scorbut et formes nouvelles,* which includes work by Raysse, Chubac, and Gilli. Raysse also takes part in several other group exhibitions in southern France.

He publishes *Poèmes*, a small book of his poetry.

1959

Raysse receives the Prix Laboratoire 32 in January.

He begins to identify himself as a *docteur* or *ingénieur de la vision*. Departing from his earlier use of discarded, derelict items, he purchases materials for his assemblages from Prisunic, a popular chain of discount stores. Anticipating Andy Warhol's prediction that "all department stores will become museums, and all museums will become department stores," Raysse announces that "the Prisunics are the museums of modern art."

The first Biennale de Paris, organized by the novelist and art theorist André Malraux, opens at the Musée d'Art moderne de la Ville de Paris in October. The exhibition marks the first public presentation of the French décollage artists Raymond Hains, Jacques de la Villeglé, and François Dufrêne.

Raysse has two solo exhibitions of paintings at Galerie Europe in Brussels and Galerie Breteau in Paris. He is included in multiple group exhibitions, among them *Poème-object* at Drian Gallery in London and the *Exposition des Artistes de France Associés* at Seletti Gallery in New York.

1960

After refusing to join the army to fight in the Algerian War, Raysse is committed to the psychiatric ward of the military hospital in Marseille, where he remains for several months.

On March 9, Klein debuts Anthropométrie de l'époque bleue *at Galerie Internationale d'Art Contemporain in Paris. To make his works, Klein coats nude women with his signature blue paint and uses their bodies as "living brushes" to spread and smear the pigment across canvas.*

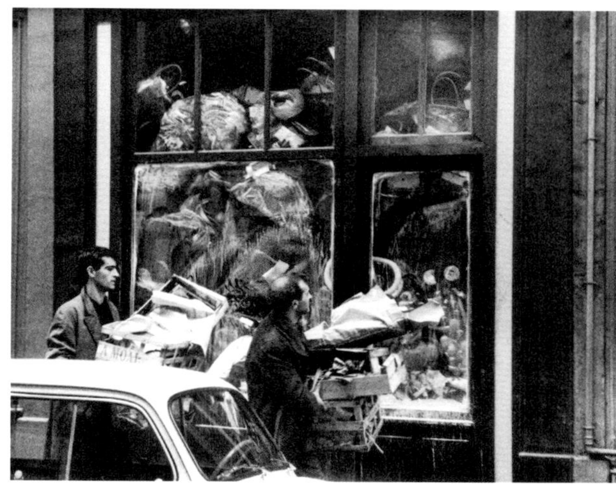

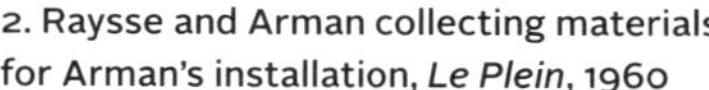
2. Raysse and Arman collecting materials for Arman's installation, *Le Plein*, 1960

Raysse moves to Paris with Arman and Klein (fig. 1).

In April, the art critic Pierre Restany organizes Nouveau Réalisme, *a group exhibition of Arman, Klein, Jean Tinguely, and the décollagists Dufrêne and Villeglé for Galleria Apollinaire in Milan. In conjunction with the exhibition, he publishes a pamphlet, "Les Nouveaux Réalistes," which serves as the group's founding statement.*

On August 22, art critic Claude Rivière publishes an article titled "La charge solaire de l'artiste" in *Combat,* a Parisian journal founded by members of the Resistance. The essay coins the term "School of Nice" to refer to artists whose work relates both visually and conceptually to the Mediterranean coast, among them Raysse, Arman, Klein, Sacha Sosnowsky (also known as Sacha Sosno), and musician Jean-Pierre Mirouze. In a 1960 interview for the Nice-based journal *Sud Communications*, Klein characterizes the group by its love of kitsch and its determination to live as if "on vacation, not in revolt."[4]

On October 23, Raysse assists Arman with his installation *Le Plein* at Galerie Iris Clert in Paris (fig. 2). In sharp rebuttal to the void of Klein's *Le Vide,* Arman fills the gallery from floor to ceiling with 250 pounds of garbage gathered from trash cans throughout the city. Raysse encourages Arman to include organic materials, such as an uncooked lobster, that cause the installation to degrade and exude a putrid odor. Viewed only through the gallery's windows, the installation comes as a caustic comment on the postwar expansion of consumer culture and its production of waste.

On October 27, Nouveau Réalisme is officially established at a meeting in Klein's studio in Paris convened by Restany. The eight artists present—Raysse, Arman, Dufrêne, Hains, Klein, Tinguely, Villeglé, and Daniel Spoerri—sign copies of a manifesto designed by Klein (fig. 3). The manifesto consists of a single sentence which, translated from French, reads: "The New Realists have become conscious of their

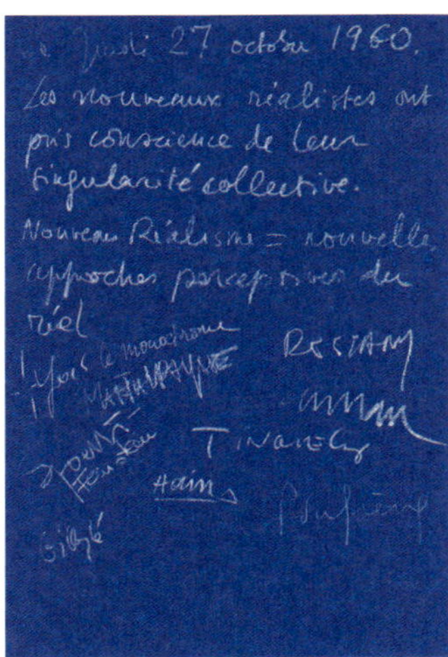

le jeudi 27 octobre 1960.
Les nouveaux réalistes ont pris conscience de leur singularité collective.
Nouveau Réalisme = nouvelles approches perceptives du réel

3. "Constitutive Declaration of New Realism" signed by original members of the Nouveaux Réalistes, 1960

collective identity; New Realism = new perceptions of the real." The group would soon be joined by César, Christo, Gérard Deschamps, Mimmo Rotella, and Niki de Saint Phalle. Reacting against the Art Informel style then dominant in Paris, the group seeks to redefine "realism" for their post-war moment, incorporating lived time, found objects, and quotidian actions into their work.

Raysse is included in several group exhibitions in France, including *Groupe de janvier* at the Galerie Bellechasse, the Salon des Réalités Nouvelles at the Musée municipal d'art moderne, and the Salon de la jeune sculpture at the Musée Rodin in Paris.

1961

Raysse meets Robert Rauschenberg in Paris.

In April, Raysse and Arman exhibit together at Galleria Schwarz in Milan. Raysse's assemblages, which enclose found items in Plexiglas cases, are shown alongside Arman's *Poubelles,* which encase garbage within plastic boxes. But while Arman makes use of discards, Raysse—continuing his focus on mass-market consumerism—purchases his objects new at the supermarket. As he later explained: "I felt the need to found a new moral attitude which would not speculate...on cellular deterioration, on the degrading conditions of man and objects doomed to decrepitude. I wanted a new world, disinfected, pure, using techniques on the same level as the technological discoveries of the modern world."[5] In his essay for the catalogue, Restany deems Arman a "humorist of the waste land" and Raysse an "ingénue of department stores."[6]

Restany organizes the exhibition *À 40° au-dessus de Dada* at Galerie J in Paris, which runs from May to June. His catalogue essay, which becomes Nouveau Réalisme's second manifesto, emphasizes the group's debt to the readymades of Duchamp and the anti-art gestures of Dada. "The New Realists consider the world a painting, the large, fundamental work from which they appropriate fragments of universal significance. They allow us to see the real in diverse aspects of its expressive totality," he writes.[7]

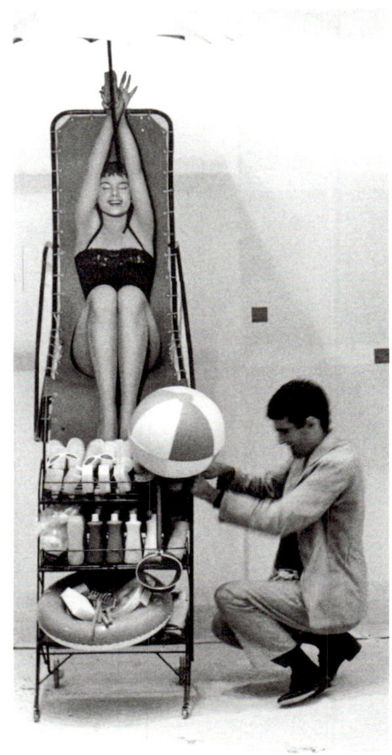

4. Raysse installing *Hygiène de la Vision no. 7* at the second Paris Biennale, 1961

Raysse participates in the first Festival des Nouveaux Réalistes at Galerie Muratore in Nice. He exhibits *La Jungle,* his first installation to depict seaside leisure. He will explore this theme further in several subsequent installations of *Raysse Beach.*

Restany organizes Le Nouveau Réalisme à Paris et à New York *at Galerie Rive Droite in Paris. Emphasizing the transatlantic reach of assemblage as an art form, the exhibition features Arman, César, Hains, Klein, Saint-Phalle, and Tinguely alongside Americans Lee Bontecou, Chryssa, John Chamberlain, Jasper Johns, Rauschenberg, and Richard Stankiewicz. Securing the visibility of New Realism in New York, the show underscores the artists' shared critique of their contemporary societies of spectacle and consumption.*

Raysse shows *Hygiène de la Vision no. 7* at the second Biennale de Paris in September. The assemblage takes the form of a publicity display dedicated to Ambre Solaire, a line of makeup products. Consisting of a photograph of a fashion model on a beach chair surrounded by plastic beach accoutrements, it is mistaken for an actual display of products and thrown away (fig. 4).

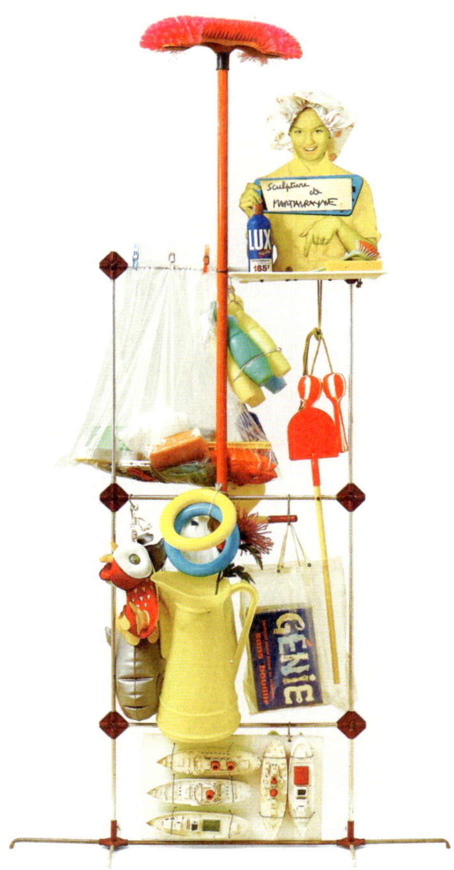

5. *Etalage, hygiène de la vision*, 1960. Assemblage of various objects, 82 ¹¹⁄₁₆ × 31 ½ × 15 ¾ inches (210 × 80 × 40 cm). Private collection

On October 2, *The Art of Assemblage* opens at the Museum of Modern Art in New York. Raysse shows *Nécropole, luxe, et parfum* (1960): a five-foot-tall plastic column containing an array of store-bought items, including cosmetics, radio parts, medicinal pills, a ping-pong ball, a toothbrush, and an artificial rose.

On October 8, Klein gathers together the members of Nouveau Réalisme, the art critics Alain Jouffroy and Pierre Descargues, and the poet John Ashbery at his apartment to discuss Restany's connection of the group to Duchamp, a filiation to which Klein objects. That evening at La Coupole, Klein, Hains, and Raysse sign a declaration that announces the group's dissolution. The group, however, continues its collective activities.

Raysse gradually abandons the aesthetic of Nouveau Réalisme for that of American Pop art, for which he feels a greater affinity. Restany later describes him as the "most autonomous, the most independent, the most anxious to remain aloof" of the group.

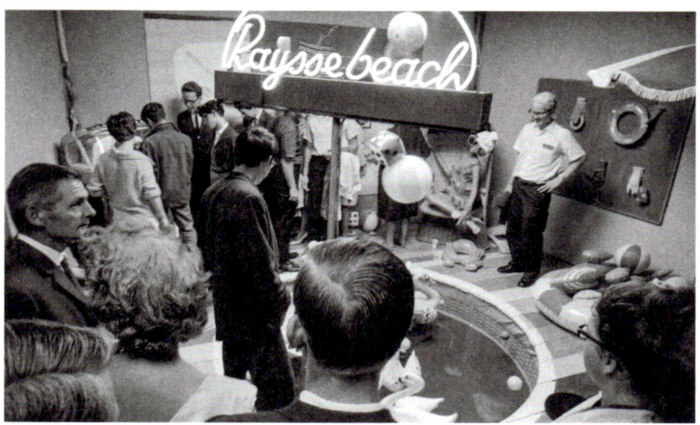

6. Installation view of *Raysse Beach* in *Dynamisch Labyrinth* (known as *Dylaby*), Stedelijk Museum, Amsterdam, 1962

1962

On June 22, Raysse debuts new work, based on stock images of the female face taken from advertisements, publicity stills, and fashion photographs, at Galerie Schmela in Dusseldorf. He creates the portraits using aerosol spray paint in lieu of more traditional artists' paints, and shows his assemblage, *Etalage, Hygiène de la Vision* (fig. 5). As he later explained: "The photo played for me the role of a connection, which in its beginning took the shape of stereotyped faces of the young women in advertisements, leitmotifs of our visual culture. Through these faces, a first type of real communication was established using ready-made formulas."[8]

In July, Warhol debuts his Campbell's Soup Cans *at Ferus Gallery in Los Angeles. Propped on makeshift shelves, the paintings, in their content and mode of display, resemble products in a supermarket.*

In August, the Stedelijk Museum mounts *Dylaby*, a "dynamic labyrinth" created through a succession of site-specific environments, each of which involves its viewers as active participants. Raysse exhibits alongside Rauschenberg, Spoerri, Saint Phalle, Tinguely, and the Finnish artist Per Olof Ultvedt. He contributes an early iteration of *Raysse Beach*, complete with a neon sign, sand, inflatable pool, artificial palm trees, mannequins, and radiant heat lamps. The installation marks his first use of neon, which will become an important material in his practice (fig. 6).

Walter Hopps's exhibition, New Paintings of Common Objects, *opens on September 25 at the Pasadena Art Museum. The first museum survey of American Pop art, it features Jim Dine, Roy Lichtenstein, Warhol, Ed Ruscha, and Wayne Thiebaud, among others.*

On October 31, *The New Realists* opens at Sidney Janis Gallery in New York. Co-organized by Restany and Janis, the show brings together nearly 30 American and European artists, including Raysse, Arman, Klein, Lichtenstein, and Warhol. Raysse contributes *Supermarket (Hygiène de la vision)* (1961), a display case filled with brushes, moisturizers, and

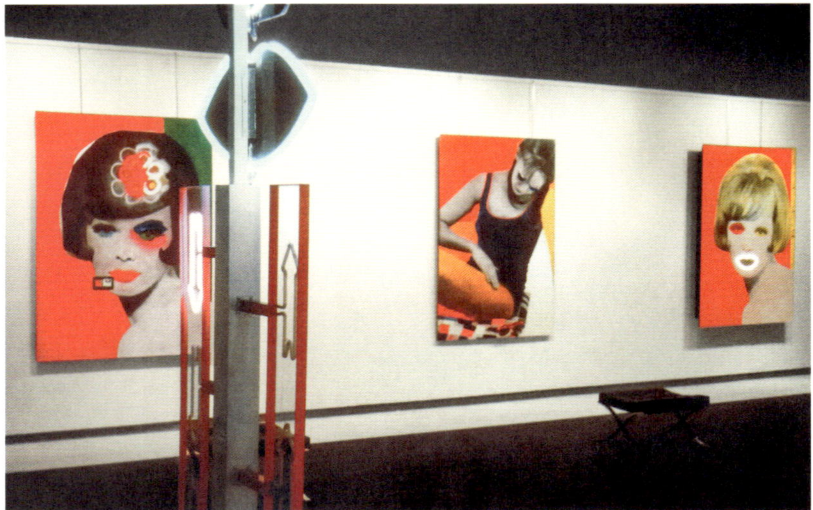

7. Installation view of *Mirrors and Portraits*, Dwan Gallery, Los Angeles, 1963

other toiletries. The show's blatantly figurative content infuriates members of the Abstract Expressionist generation, such as Robert Motherwell, Mark Rothko, Philip Guston, and Adolph Gottlieb, who quit Janis's gallery in protest.

A modified version of *Raysse Beach* is restaged in the artist's first solo exhibition at Alexander Iolas Gallery in New York. Ashbery praises it as a "terse homage to the pleasures of plastic."

Raysse joins the artistic community that gathers at the Chelsea Hotel. Along with Arman, Saint Phalle, and Tinguely, he socializes with Claes Oldenburg, Rauschenberg, and Chamberlain.

Raysse has solo exhibitions in New York and Dusseldorf and is featured in several group exhibitions in the United States and Europe, including *Anti-peinture / Avant-garde international* at Galerie Hessenhuis in Antwerp and the Salon Comparaisons at the Musée d'Art moderne de la Ville de Paris.

1963

Raysse visits Los Angeles, where he will return many times through 1968.

In January, his exhibition, *Mirrors and Portraits,* opens at Dwan Gallery in Los Angeles (fig. 7). The catalogue features a text by Ashbery. "Martial Raysse has taken the colors and textures of this attractive world of the supermarket and made a poem of them. The colors are the lurid pastel and fluorescent ones of useful articles; the textures are those of aluminum, plastic, and nylon," he writes.[9]

Raysse begins to use Xerox photocopies in his work.

The De Young Museum in San Francisco presents a solo exhibition of Raysse's work, and he is included in several group exhibitions in the United States and Europe.

1964

Raysse begins his Made in Japan series, in which he distorts Old Master paintings by Jean-Auguste-Dominique Ingres, Lucas Cranach the Elder, and Jacopo Tintoretto, among others (page 19). This new series is shown in the exhibition *Made in Japan... Tableau horrible... Tableau de mauvais goût...* at Alexander Iolas Gallery in New York, and at the gallery's Paris location the following year. Rendered in a vibrant palette that he terms "Martialcolor," the series highlights its ironic deviation from the originals, delighting in what Raysse extols as its self-consciously "bad taste." In the catalogue accompanying the show, Restany writes: "Raysse's nature prodigally pours forth the continual glitter of its tinseled riches, its pearls of neon, its decorative vegetation, the luxury of its villas, the mellow sensuality of its sunlight, the subdued blue of its sky and sea. This nature has been sophisticated to excess—what the travel promoters would call its enhancement—and here lies the secret of its real beauty."[10]

Raysse begins to use flocking, a technique in which he sprays plasticized material directly onto the surface of his canvases, lending them a pronounced sense of texture and tactility.

He makes his first film, *Suzanna, Suzanna.* Removing the elders from Tintoretto's *Susanna and the Elders,* he overlays the gap with a film of Arman dressed in a fake beard and white robe.

Raysse is featured in the group exhibition *Boxes* at Virginia Dwan Gallery in Los Angeles, in which Andy Warhol first exhibits his Brillo Boxes.

He participates in several group exhibitions organized by European museums.

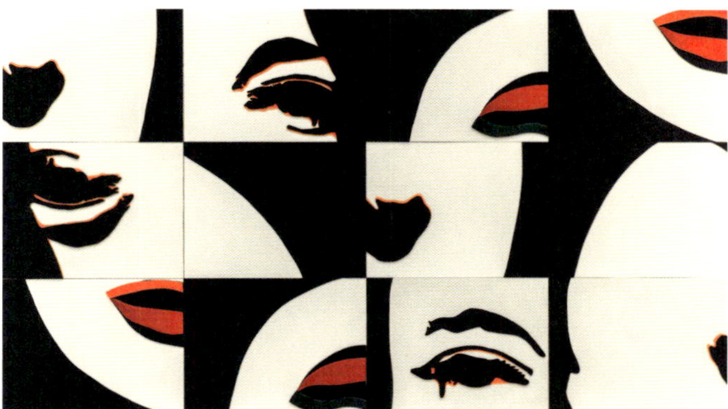

8. *Life is so complex*, 1966. Opaque and transparent colored Plexiglas cut and mounted on plywood, 59 ¼ × 102 ⅜ × 1 ¾ inches (150.5× 260× 4.6 cm). Collection Musée de Grenoble

1965

He continues his engagement with portraiture, melding it with a reflection on the object quality of the picture and frame. Creating "broken," "folded," "rolled-up," and "convex pictures," he begins to deconstruct his images into figurative units that will become increasingly autonomous (fig. 8).

In October his first retrospective, *Martial Raysse, Master and Slave of the Imagination,* opens at the Stedelijk Museum in Amsterdam. The catalogue includes an introduction by Restany and an essay by art critic Otto Hahn. Raysse also contributes a text, in which he proclaims his taste for "bad taste." "Clumsiness is touching because it breaks the rules of the game in search of true feeling. I have sought life in color through plastic, fluorescence, neon, artificial lighting and now false relationships, disharmony, awful, unsuccessfully, badly made pictures with mistakes, bad taste, the horrible, and last but not least what is artificial," he writes.[11]

Raysse's work is included in group exhibitions in Europe and the United States, including *Current Art* at the Institute of Contemporary Art at the University of Pennsylvania and *Arena of Love* at Dwan Gallery in Los Angeles.

1966

With Saint Phalle and Tinguely, he creates the sets for Roland Petit's ballet, *L'Eloge de la folie,* which is staged in March at the Théâtre des Champs-Elysées in Paris. His contribution interrupts the rhythm of the ballet with vivid colors and light projections.

In November, he shows his "variable geometry" paintings at Alexander Iolas Gallery in New York. Composed of multiple panels, the works speak to what Hahn describes as the "compartmentalized and partial" nature of modern vision, forcing the viewer to piece together dispersed images. He continues: "For Raysse, it is not a question of doing a painting that looks like a prairie or a portrait, but of inventing a new substitute for the prairie or the portrait: photo, photocopy, flocking, paper cutting, neon...Anything at all, as long as it shatters identity and widens the distance from reality. Raysse wants to stay in the realm of illusion, of dream."[12]

Chosen to represent France at the Venice Biennale, Raysse contributes *Nice-Venice,* a polyptych of 30 panels that simulates a visual journey between the two cities. Installed at oblique angles, the work presents a distorted and oneiric vision of the Mediterranean coast.

He publishes a manifesto in the journal *Collage*, in which he critiques the current state of painting and outlines the need for an artistic vision that reflects contemporary realities. "The so-called painting of the present is nothing but a layer of fossils peacefully building up a transition stage that has no connection with the life we are living.... Painting begins tomorrow. It will be the work of young artists that are to come," he declares.[13]

He encounters the experimental cinema of Kenneth Anger, Stan Brakhage, and Glauber Rocha, which he views along with the films of Jean-Luc Godard and Pierre Perrault. He makes the short film *Jésus-Cola*, which he describes as a "paranoid critique of consumer society."

Raysse participates in several group exhibitions internationally.

1967

Raysse collaborates again with Petit, creating the sets for his ballet *Paradise Lost,* which is staged in February at Covent Garden in London. Based on the story of Genesis, the ballet's scenery consists of variable geometric elements mounted on mobile aluminum panels and accented with neon.

In July, he experiments with cinematic effects at the Research Unit of the Office de Radiodiffusion-Télévision Française (ORTF). His film, *Portrait Electro Machin Chose,* makes use of solarization and other techniques of color distortion, exploring the possibilities of high-contrast and false pigmentation alongside superimposition and transparency.

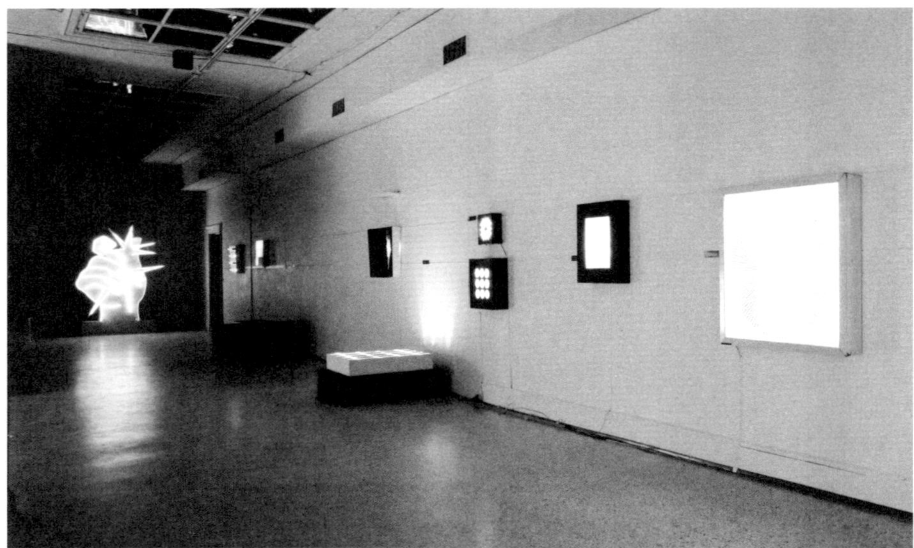

9. Installation view of the group exhibition *Light, Motion, Space*, Walker Art Center, Minneapolis, 1967; at far left, Raysse's *America, America*, 1964

With Marcel Hanoun, he participates in the French section of the fourth Festival of Experimental Film at Knokke-le-Zoute (EXPRMNTL 4), held in Belgium from December through February of the following year.

Solo exhibitions of his work are held internationally, including a retrospective at the Palais des beaux-arts in Brussels.

Raysse is included in *Light, Motion, Space*, one of the first museum exhibitions of Kinetic art, which debuts at the Walker Art Center in Minneapolis and travels to the Milwaukee Art Center. Curated by Willoughby Sharp, the exhibition features forty-two artists, including Günther Uecker, Julio Le Parc, and Nam June Paik (fig. 9).

Among other group exhibitions, Galerie de la Salle features Raysse in *Ecole de Nice?*.

1968

His refusal to take part in the Marzotto Prize in Milan signals his increasing rift with the official art world. He publishes an open letter in the journal *Robho*, explaining his objections to juried competitions for art and affirming the nature of his artistic approach which seeks, in his words, "to transform vision on the basis of immediate elements of objective experience."[14]

Disillusioned with the American art world, he returns to Paris amid the civil unrest and student-led protests of May 1968. A self-proclaimed *homme de gauche*, he joins the Atelier Populaire at the Ecole de Beaux-Arts, where he assists in its collective poster-making in support of political radicalism.

Inspired by the collaborative spirit of the Atelier Populaire, he realizes *Riverside D tout seul Ankammon*, a small brochure of Surrealist-inspired "exquisite corpse" drawings by himself and several other artists and filmmakers.

Raysse has solo exhibitions at the Museum of Contemporary Art in Chicago and other institutions. He participates in several group exhibitions, including *12 Environments* at the Kunsthalle in Bern.

1969

Raysse begins his series Formes en liberté, which he creates in media ranging from corrugated cardboard and papier-mâché to film projections. Debuting the series at Galerie Alexander Iolas in Paris, Raysse links the concept to Proxima Centauri, the nearest star to our solar system, as an allegory for his declared departure from the official art world. He writes: "In my reflection on the evolution of the form I have tried to release it from the frame, then from the support, and finally from any contingency. Here its image from the projector is visible and retained on the ceiling, nothing stops me from following it in its course to the place from which it proceeds in me: PROXIMA CENTAURI."[15]

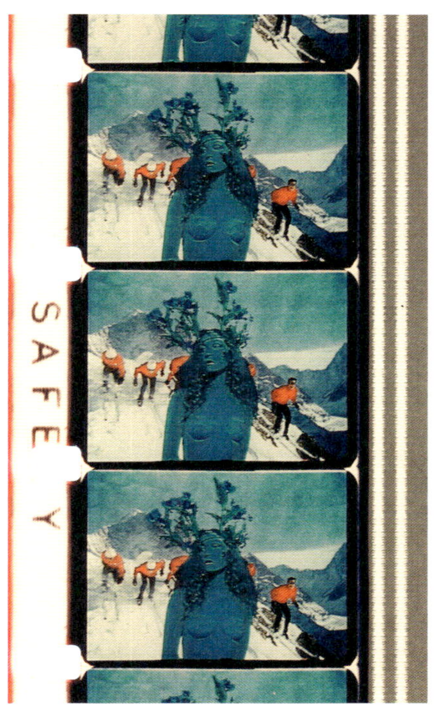

10. Film frames from *Camembert Martial Extra-Doux*, 1969. Collection Musée National d'Art Moderne, Centre Georges Pompidou

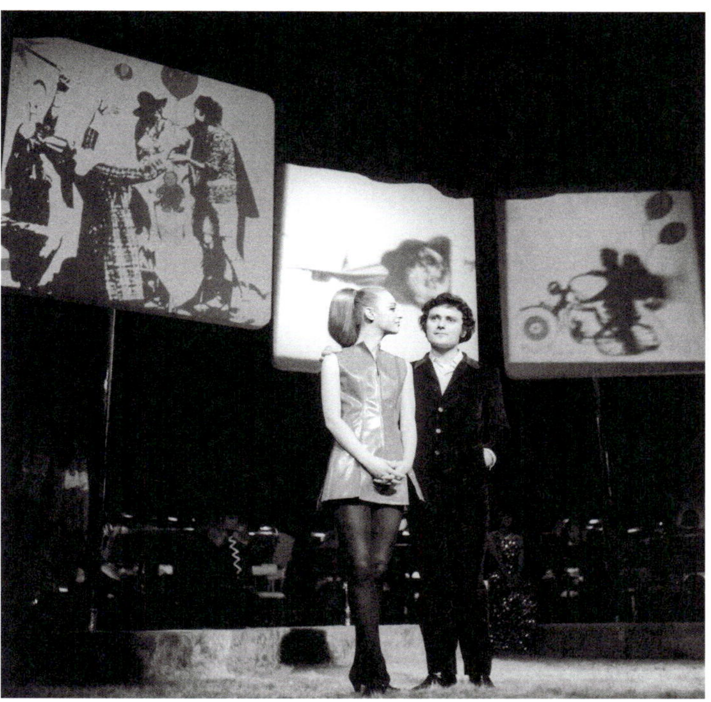

11. Performance of *Votre Faust* with set design by Martial Raysse, Teatro alla Scala, Milan, 1969

He creates a series of cardboard and wood assemblages that adopt the morphemes "x," "y," "z," and the star, which will become central elements of his aesthetic vocabulary.

He makes a short film, *Camembert Martial Extra-Doux,* about a family of peasants who eat the cheese named in its title and discover that it possesses hallucinogenic properties (fig. 10).

He designs the scenery for Henri Pousseur and Michel Butor's opera *Votre Faust*, presented at Teatro alla Scala in Milan (fig. 11).

After breaking with his gallery for political reasons amidst the 1968 protests, he is selected by the students of the Ecole nationale supérieure des Arts Décoratifs in Paris to be a professor. He chooses to teach at night to make the class more accessible, and meets often with 35 to 40 students at his home in Paris. Disillusioned with the critical discourse around his work, he feels rejuvenated through teaching and later recalls this period as a new beginning.

Raysse participates in several solo and group exhibitions internationally, including *Peintres européens d'aujourd'hui/ European Painters Today* at the Jewish Museum in New York, and *Electromagica* at the Japan Electric Art Association in Tokyo.

1970

Raysse abandons painting for a variety of new media and forms. As he later reflects: "Naively, when I started, I thought that painting would be enough. But the logical development of the picture is the slide, the magazine, the screen, the total spectacle."[16]

He shoots his first feature-length film, *Le grand départ* (1972) in Morocco and Paris. Chronicling a community outside the norms of society, the film is both a voyage into the depths of the self and an epic intergalactic exploration. Abounding in literary and visual allusions, it references Eugene Delacroix, Théodore Géricault, Jean-Auguste-Dominique Ingres, and the travel narratives of Xavier de Maistre in delirious, proliferating allegories.

He designs his first periodical cover for the magazine *20 ans*.

In October, Nouveau Réalisme celebrates its tenth anniversary. To mark the occasion Restany organizes a group exhibition in Milan, for which Raysse shows several films and projects *Formes en liberté* on the city's Duomo.

Raysse's work is shown in several solo exhibitions, including *Une forme en liberté* at Alexander Iolas Gallery and *Hygiène de la Vision* at Galleria del Leone in Venice. His work is also included in *Pop Art*, presented at the 23rd Belgian Summer Festival.

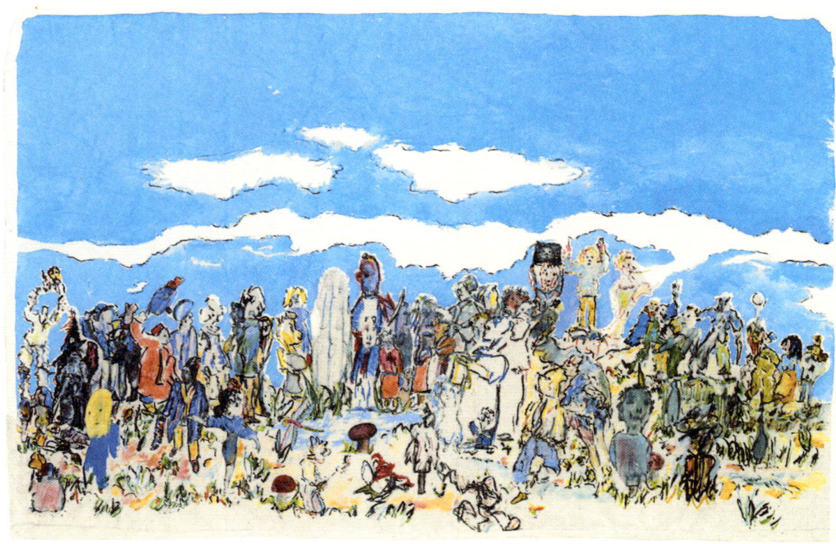

12. *Loco Bello - Image X*, 1975–76. Pastel, distemper, collage on paper mounted on cardboard, Plexiglas box, 52 ¾ × 79 ⅛ inches (134 × 201 cm). Collections Karmitz

1971

In preparation for the 1972 Olympic Games in Munich, architect Paolo Nestler designs a series of mobile structures for the Haus der Kunst that are used to house a "living museum" of exhibitions and performances. Within this space Raysse creates *Oued Laou*. Named after a small village in northern Morocco, the work consists of a desert scene on which Raysse projects "free forms" of magic-lantern images, accompanied by a soundtrack of birdsongs and animal cries.

Raysse withdraws from autonomous artistic activities to pursue collective work. He joins the artists' commune PIG and anonymously produces the review *Pig Music*, a playful publication that recounts these experiences of collective creation.

He stars in Jean-Pierre Prévost's feature film, *Jupiter*.

In May, Raysse presents a solo exhibition of *Oued Laou* at the Pinakothek der Moderne in Munich. His work is included in *Le Bain turc d'Ingres*, a group exhibition at the Louvre.

1972

He presents *Six images calmes* at Galerie Alexandre Iolas in Paris. The exhibition elaborates essential elements of Raysse's visual vocabulary—the outline of a head, the star, the cross, and the final letters of the Latin alphabet—in different media and materials, including silkscreen prints, plastic, neon, and film projections. The gallery's Milan location presents *Cari Amici. Martial Raysse* in April.

1973

He moves to Ussy-sur-Marne in Seine-et-Marne. Inspired by the region's bucolic landscape, he begins Loco Bello, a series of paintings and drawings populated by fantastical creatures amid lush vegetation (fig. 12).

Raysse's work is included in the group exhibition *L'Art du 20e siècle dans les collections genevoises*, held at the Musée Rath in Geneva.

1974

Raysse's brother, Gilles, rents a small storefront on Rue du Dragon in Paris. Here, Raysse stages a guerilla exhibition, *Coco Mato,* presenting a series of assemblages that he had been developing since 1970. Taking its title from the Italian slang for Amanita muscaria, a red-and-white spotted mushroom known for its psychedelic effects, the show features fantastical constructions of leaves, pins, feathers, shells, figurines, plastic, and other everyday materials, which resemble mystical fetishes.

1975

In March, Galerie Benador in Geneva holds a solo exhibition of Raysse's work, *Sic transit Gloria mundi.*

In November, Raysse presents a solo exhibition at Galerie Der Spiegel in Cologne, titled *Neue Bilder und Zeichnungen*.

1976

He makes the short film *Lotel des folles fatmas*.

In May, Galerie Karl Flinker in Paris opens *Loco Bello – images récentes*, an exhibition of Raysse's work.

He participates in the 37th Venice Biennale.

Raysse's work is shown in *Boîtes*, a group exhibition at the Musée d'Art moderne de la Ville de Paris.

1977

He begins his Spelunca series: large-scale, figurative compositions inspired by *The Dream of Poliphilus*, an early Renaissance allegory of courtly love first published in Venice in 1499, featuring elegant woodcut illustrations. Art critic Gilbert Lascault writes: "Curiously, these images do not astonish or shock us. Raysse does not want to surprise us. He offers us scenes that appear strangely familiar. They refer to our myths. They play around with our cultures. They evoke, in our fantasies, the bacchanalia painted by Nicolas Poussin.... The painter here is on the side of a logic of forms and colors: a logic that excludes symbolic discourse: a logic that then prevents us from even being able to formulate its rules."[17]

Solo exhibitions of Raysse's work are held at Galerie Eva de Buren in Stockholm and at the Centre d'art in Flaine.

Raysse participates in two group exhibitions at the Centre Pompidou: *A propos de Nice* and *Paris-New York*.

His work is shown at Documenta 6 in Kassel.

1978

His exhibition *Spelunca nouvelles images* opens in October at Galerie Karl Flinker in Paris.

Raysse's work is included in the 12th Biennale internationale de Menton.

1979

He moves to Dordogne in the southwest of France, where he paints a series of small pictures titled La Petite Maison.

Raysse is included in several group exhibitions, including the 3rd Biennale of Sydney, held at the Art Gallery of New South Wales.

1980

In an allusion to antique statuary, he begins to incorporate stone paste into his works. Of his increasing engagement with large-scale sculpture, he comments: "Long reflection on archetypes has led me from painting to sculpture. From reflection on painting, I've take a form that has become an object, freed from the space of the frame...It is a sculpture."[18]

Solo exhibitions of his work are held at Galerie Glaude Givaudan in Geneva and Stichting Veranneman, Kruishoutem in Belgium. He participates in group exhibitions at Galerie Karl Flinker and the Maison des arts in Montbéliard.

1981

An exhibition at the Centre Pompidou in Paris traces the prior ten years of his work. In the catalogue, curator Pontus Hultén writes of the artist's paintings: "The color glows, shoots off sparks and blazes in a way we have never seen it do in Renoir. It is suddenly clear that the feeling of happiness can perhaps be expressed and conveyed more easily with colors than by any other means. Raysse has proved it. He is capable of putting us in a real state of drunkenness and enchantment. Thanks to his painting, painting is a dream."[19]

He makes the video portrait *Sous un arbre perché* for the series *Les Peintres cinéastes*, organized by Jean-Michel Arnold for the Centre national de la recherche scientifique (CNRS) in Paris.

Opening in October, a solo exhibition titled *Gouaches en objecten* is presented at the Stedelijk Museum in Amsterdam.

1982

He creates a suite of monumental sculptures, *Les Chemins de la Liberté*, which allude to the French Revolution.

He is awarded the Grand Prix National de la Peinture in December.

Raysse has a solo exhibition at the Musée Picasso in Antibes.

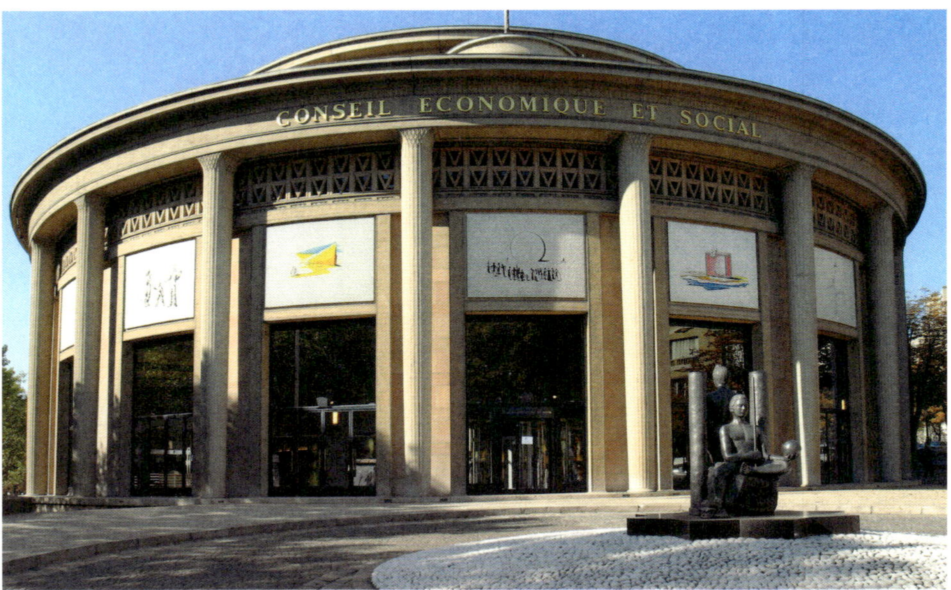

13. Conseil économique et social, Paris, with sculpture and mosaics designed by Raysse

Among several group exhibitions, he is included in the 40th Venice Biennale, and in *'60–'80 attitudes/concepts/images. Een keuze uit twintig jaar beeldende kunst. A selection from Twenty Years of Visual Arts* at the Stedelijk Museum in Amsterdam.

1983

Raysse's work is included in a group exhibition commemorating the anniversary of Picasso's death. *Bonjour Monsieur Picasso: 13 commandes du Musée d'Antibes à des artistes pour le 10e anniversaire de la mort de Picasso, 1973–avril–1983: Adami, Alechinsky, Arman, Bioules, César, Equipo Crónica, Erro, Folon, Guttuso, Messagier, Pignon, Raysse, Saura* is held at the Musée Picasso in Antibes.

1984

He participates in group exhibitions, including *The Becht Collection: Visual Art from the Agnes and Frits Becht Collection*, presented in March at the Stedelijk Museum, and *Peinture non plane en France d'aujourd'hui*, which opens at Galerie Fernand Léger, Ivry-sur-Seine, in May.

1985

At the Nouvelle Biennale de Paris, Raysse shows his Graal series, a suite of five paintings accompanied by an enigmatic phrase that reads, in French: "For the right measure in the double world and pure knowledge of love through Monsalvat to the Grail."[20]

Raysse participates in several group exhibitions, including *Depuis Matisse, la couleur dans l'art français*, held at the Palais des beaux-arts in Brussels.

1986

He meets François Pinault, who will become a principal collector of his work.

The Musée d'art moderne de la Ville de Paris features Raysse's work in the exhibition *1960, les Nouveaux Réalistes*.

The Vancouver Art Gallery includes Raysse's work in the exhibition *Luxe, calme et volupté: aspects of French Art, 1966–1986: Daniel Buren, Robert Combas, Robert Filliou, Gérard Garouste, Pierre Klossowski, Jean Le Gac, Annette Messager, Martial Raysse*. He is included in several other group exhibitions worldwide.

1987

In February, the Bhirasri Institute of Modern Art in Bangkok features Raysse's work in a group exhibition titled *Peintures en France: les années 80 – French Painting of the 1980s*.

1988

With the Italian sculptor Vito Tongiani, he creates *La Fontaine de la place du Marché* in Nîmes, a large-scale marble work consisting of a truncated column and a crocodile.

An exhibition of Raysse's work is presented at Galleria Claudio Botello Arte in Turin. He participates in an exhibition on Nouveau Réalisme at Galerie Zabrinskie in New York.

1989

Raysse designs a monumental work for the Conseil économique et social, Place d'Iéna in Paris. It consists of a bronze statuary group and eleven mosaic panels executed by master mosaicist Luigi Guardigli (fig. 13).

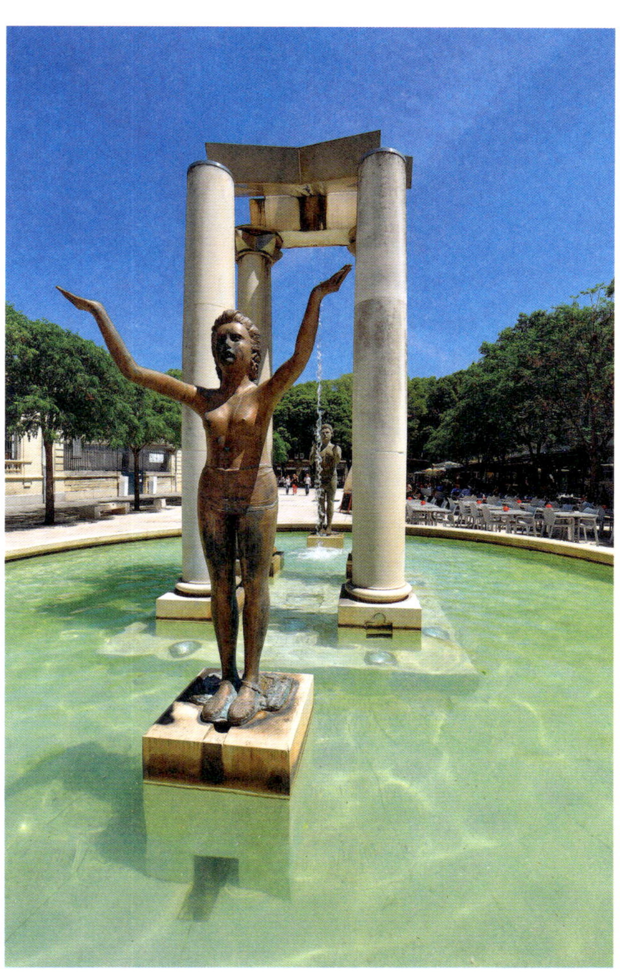

14. Fountain designed by Martial Raysse, Place d'Assas, Nîmes

Raysse designs a second fountain in Nîmes that is inaugurated in Place d'Assas. It includes two large stone heads representing the patron detities of the city, Nemausus and Nemausa, from whom Nîmes takes its name. Water flows from their mouths into a central pool, where two bronze figures representing day and night stand on either side of four stone columns supporting a large metal star (fig. 14).

Raysse presents solo exhibitions in Cologne and Paris, and his work is included in *Estampes et Révolution, 200 ans après* at the Centre national des artes plastiques in Paris.

1990

In honor of the French Revolution, he creates *Liberté chérie*, a classically inspired figure. He will produce several versions in different media, including cast bronze and aluminum.

Galerie Montaigne in Paris includes Raysse's work in an exhibition about Virginia Dwan's involvement with Nouveau Réalisme. The Fondation Electricité de France features his art in the exhibition *Nature (artificielle)* along with the work of more than a dozen of his contemporaries, including Pier Paolo Calzolari, Dan Flavin, Jenny Holzer, Mario Merz, François Morellet, and James Turrell.

1991

Raysse makes the monumental bronze statue *Rik de Hop la Houppe*, based on Charles Perrault's fairytale.

He participates in several group exhibitions, including the Quindicesima Biennale Internationale del Bronzetto Piccola Scultura at the Palazzo della Ragione in Padua.

1992

He paints the large-scale composition *Le Carnaval à Périgueux* (page 17), which combines imagery from Shakespeare's *A Midsummer Night's Dream* with allusions to the present day.

Among other solo exhibitions, the Galerie nationale du Jeu de Paume mounts a comprehensive retrospective of Raysse's work.

His work is featured in several group exhibitions, including Documenta 9 in Kassel, the French Pavilion at the Universal Exposition in Seville, and the group exhibition *Le portrait dans l'art contemporain, 1945–1992* at the Musée d'art moderne et d'art contemporain in Nice.

1993

A solo exhibition of his work, titled *Pour l'autres vacandes...*, is held at the Carré d'art – Musée d'art contemporain in Nîmes.

1994

Raysse participates in the group exhibitions *Le modèle, le double, l'identique* at the Musée de Picardie in Amiens and *Collection particulière* at the Galerie de France in Paris

1995

Raysse begins a series of frescoes for a chapel in Pierrefeu, France, which are not installed.

In October, his work is included in the group exhibition *Féminin-Masculin. Le sexe de l'art* at the Centre Pompidou in Paris. It features a diverse group of artists, including Marina Abramovic and Ulay, Louise Bourgeois, Marcel Duchamp, Gilbert and George, Eva Hesse, Jasper Johns, Frida Kahlo, Robert Mapplethorpe, François Morellet, Jackson Pollock, and Andy Warhol, among others.

1996

Raysse unveils *Mais dites une seule parole*, a sweeping allegorical painting commissioned for the François-Mitterand Library at the Bibliothèque national de France.

A solo exhibition of his work is held at the Galerie de France in Paris, and he participates in group exhibitions in Italy and France.

1997

He makes several drawings on the theme of Bacchus.

Martial Raysse. Promenade avec vue sur Bacchus, le pain et le vin is shown at the Maison des arts Georges Pompidou in Cajarc. The artist writes an accompanying text, which features one of his Bacchus drawings on the cover. (fig. 15; text in English and French, pages 24–27).

The Centre Pompidou mounts the exhibition *Martial Raysse. Chemin faisant, Frère Crayon et Sainte Gomme.*

His work is featured in several group exhibitions, including a presentation of French art at the Museo Tamayo in Mexico City.

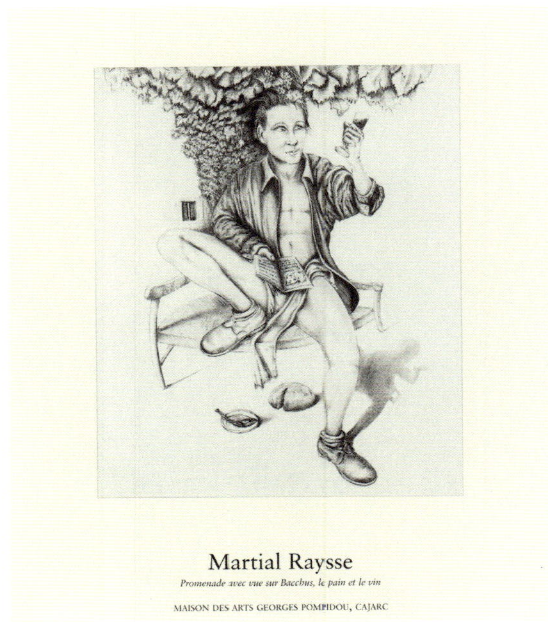

15. Cover of *Martial Raysse. Promenade avec vue sur Bacchus, le pain et le vin*, published by the Maison des arts George Pompidou, Cajarc, 1997

1998

Raysse presents a solo exhibition at the Palais Liechtenstein in Vienna.

His work is included in *De Klein à Warhol, face à face France/Etats-Unis: collections du Musée national d'art moderne et du Musée d'art moderne et d'art contemporain de Nice* at the Musée d'art moderne et d'art contemporain in Nice.

1999

He makes drawings for the Chapel of Saint-Martial in Ribérac, France.

The Espace culturel François Mitterrand in Périgueux debuts his large-scale work *Le Carnival à Périgueux* in a solo exhibition.

The Museum of Modern Art in New York features Raysse in the group exhibition *Pop Impressions Europe/USA: Prints and Multiples from The Museum of Modern Art, 1960–1975.*

2000

He makes the short film *Ex-voto.*

Raysse has several solo exhibitions in French museums, and at the Central Academy of Fine Arts in Beijing.

His work is included in group exhibitions in France and Japan.

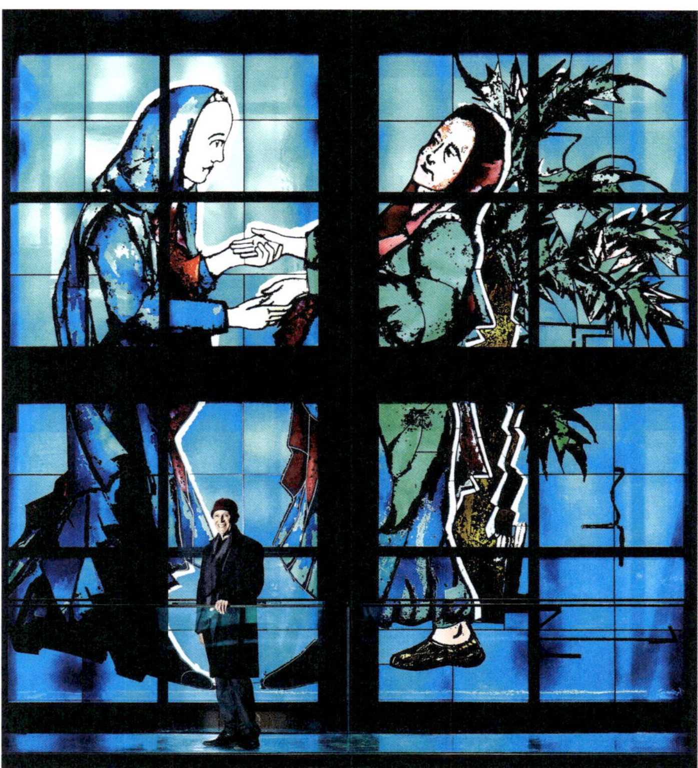

Martial Raysse in front of stained glass windows he designed for the Church of Notre-Dame de l'Arche d'Alliance, Paris, 2001

2001

He creates two stained glass windows for the Church of Notre-Dame de l'Arche d'Alliance in Paris (fig. 16).

Among other group exhibitions, Raysse participates in *Les Années Pop* at the Centre Pompidou in Paris.

2002

Raysse's work is featured in the group exhibition *Paris: Capital of the Arts,* mounted at the Royal Academy of Arts in London and shown at the Guggenheim Museum Bilbao.

2004

Raysse takes part in *Declaration: 100 Artists for Peace* at the National Museum of Contemporary Art in Seoul.

2005

He produces a portrait in neon light, *Sinéma, les anges sont avec toi*, for the façade of the MK2 Quai de Loire cinema in Paris. *Rik de Hop la Houppe* is reimagined in aluminum bronze and exhibited at the MK2 Bibliothèque.

The Galerie de France presents *Dieu merci, un tableau de Martial Raysse*, an exhibition of his work.

His work is included in a group show of contemporary French art in the collection of the Centre Pompidou, which travels to Shanghai, Guangzhou, and Beijing.

2006

Raysse participates in the exhibitions *La Force de l'art*, held at the Grand Palais in Paris, and *Le noir est une couleur—Hommage vivant à Aimé Maeght* at the Fondation Marguerite et Aimé Maeght in Saint-Paul.

2007

He creates two large-scale allegorical paintings, *Heureux rivages* and *Poisson d'avril*, which continue his exploration of the carnival theme.

Raysse participates in several group exhibitions, including *Le Nouveau Réalisme* at the Palais in Paris, which travels to the Sprengel Museum in Hannover.

2008

Editions MK2 releases a boxed DVD set of the films made by Raysse between 1966 and 2008.

2009

Raysse takes part in several group exhibitions internationally. His works are shown in *I∆O – Explorations psychédéliques en France, 1968–∞* at the CAPC musée d'art contemporain in Bordeaux and *Ingres et les modernes* at the Musée national des beaux-arts du Québec.

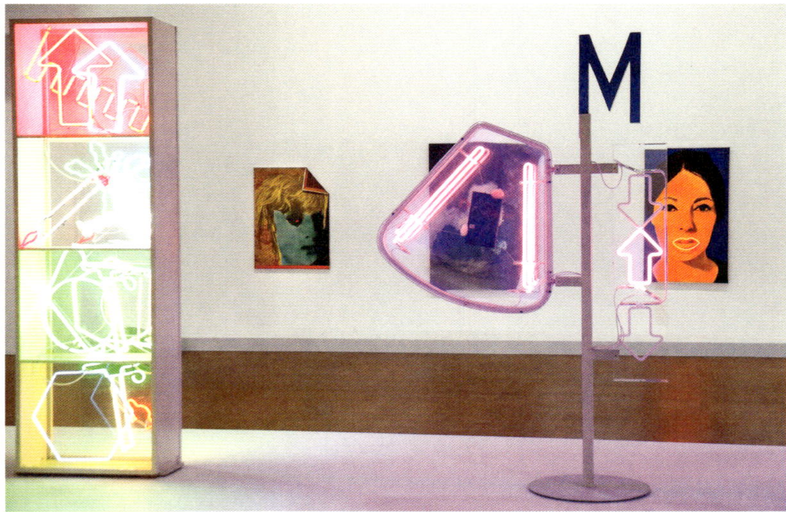

17. Installation view of *Martial Raysse*, Centre National d'Art et de Culture Georges Pompidou, Paris, 2014

2010

Raysse is part of the group exhibitions *Hope ! Une exposition d'Art contemporain sur l'espoir*, presented at the Palais des arts et du festival in Dinard, and *Nuevos realismos 1957–1962: Estrategias del objeto, entre ready-made y espectáculo* at the Museo nacional de arte Reina Sofía in Madrid.

2011

His 1964 painting *Quinze août* achieves a record price at auction, making him the most expensive living French artist at the time.

2012

He creates the large-scale picture *Ici Plage, comme ici-bas*, which continues his career-long engagement with portraiture, landscape, and history painting (page 17).

The solo exhibition *Le Studiolo. Les petits Martial Raysse dans la collection Galerie de France* is held at the Galerie de France in Paris.

His work is shown in several group exhibitions, including *Neon, Who's afraid of red, yellow and blue?* at La Maison Rouge, Fondation Antoine de Galbert in Paris.

2013

He creates a light installation, *Relebainturc*, for the lobby of the MK2 Bibliothèque in Paris.

An exhibition at Luxembourg & Dayan in New York surveys his career from 1960 to 1974.

Group exhibitions include *Pop Art Design* at the Barbican Art Gallery in London, which also features Roy Lichtenstein, Claes Oldenburg, and Andy Warhol.

2014

The Centre Pompidou organizes a major retrospective of his work (fig. 17). The catalogue of the exhibition features essays by Catherine Grenier, Françoise Viatte, Dimitri Salmon, Anaël Pigeat, and Cécile Debray, and a chronology by Mica Gherghescu.

In July, he is awarded the Praemium Imperiale by the Japan Art Association.

2015

A retrospective of his work, curated by Caroline Bourgeois, opens at Palazzo Grassi in Venice (fig. 18). The catalogue of the exhibition includes essays by Didier Semin, Andrea Bellini, Dimitri Salmon, Alison M. Gingeras, and Françoise Viatte, a transcribed conversation between Anaël Pigeat and Philippe Azoury, and a chronology by Mica Gherghescu.

2016

Galerie du Griffon holds a solo exhibition focusing on Raysse's works on paper.

2017

Kamel Mennour Gallery in Paris holds the solo exhibition *La Belle Jeanne*, which highlights his works on paper.

In Neuchâtel, Galerie du Griffon features Raysse's *France Bleue* (1964) in the group exhibition *La Nouvelle Figuration Européene: 1964–1976*.

Raysse attends the dedication of his sculpture *Ric de Hop la Houppe* at the Art Museum of Tsinghua University in Beijing.

2018

In February, *Martial Raysse: Visages* opens at Lévy Gorvy in New York.

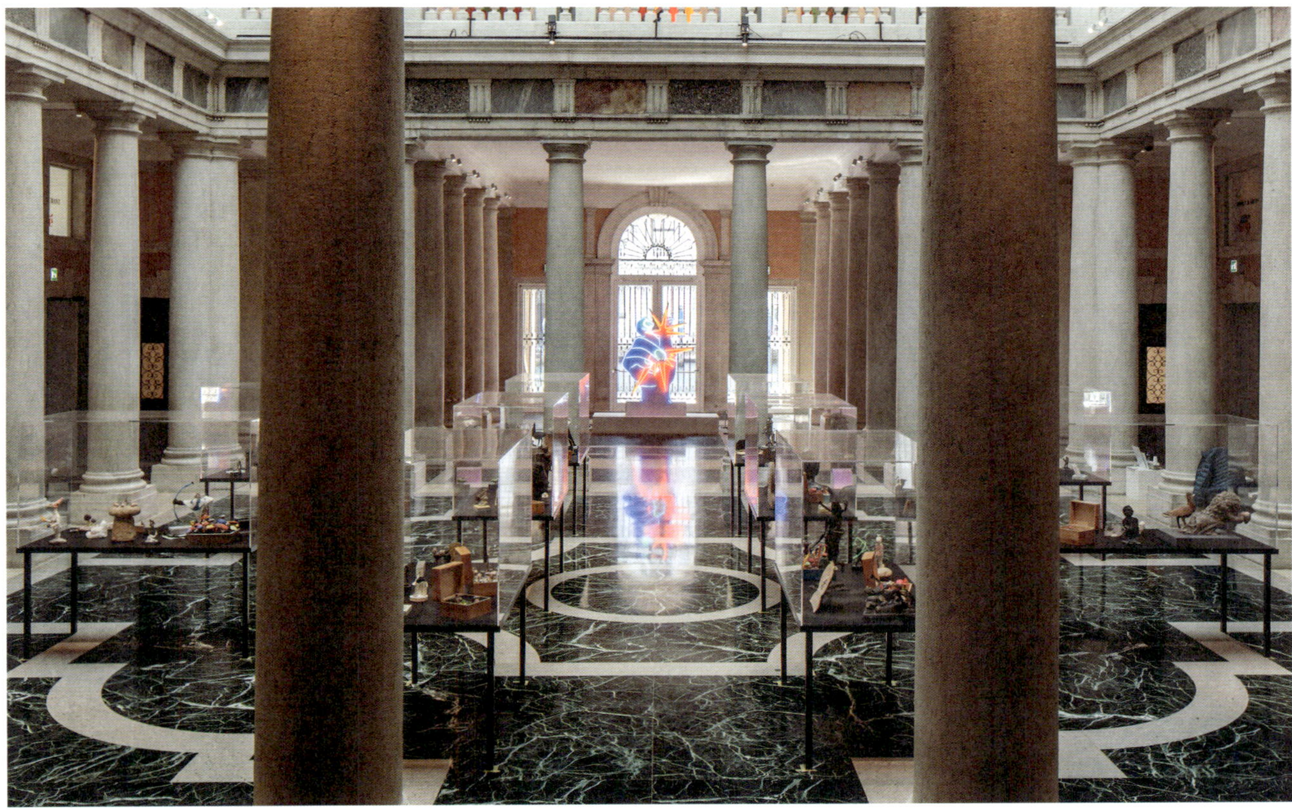

18. Installation view of *Martial Raysse*, Palazzo Grassi, Venice, 2015

1. Martial Raysse, cited in Martial Raysse, Galerie de France, Paris, February 17–March 18, 2000.

2. Martial Raysse interviewed by Guy de Belleval, "Je fais n'importe quoi, avec n'importe quoi," *Le Journal de Genève* no. 36 (February 12–13, 1966): 19. Translated in Mica Gherghescu, "Timeline," in *Martial Raysse*, exh. cat. (Venice: Marsilio Editori, 2015), 464.

3. Letter from Jean Cocteau to Martial Raysse, 1958, published in V. Dabin, "Chronologie," in *Martial Raysse*, exh. cat. (Nîmes: Galerie nationale du Jeu de Paume, 1992); Trans. Gherghescu, "Timeline," in *Martial Raysse*, 464.

4. Klein, quoted in a 1960 interview with Sacha Sosno, "Klein, Raysse, Arman: des Nouveaux Réalistes," reprinted in *Yves Klein: 3 mars–23 mai 1983* (Paris: Centre Georges Pompidou, 1983), 264.

5. Raysse, quoted in *Martial Raysse: Obrazy a Objekty, 1969* (Prague: National Gallery of Prague, 1969), n.p.

6. Pierre Restany, "Arman, Martial Raysse et le bon sens," in *Arman & Raysse: mostra collettiva*, exh. cat. (Milan: Galleria Schwarz, 1961). Trans. Gherghescu, "Timeline," in *Martial Raysse*, 467.

7. Reprinted in *Theories and Documents of Contemporary Art*, Kristine Stiles, ed.; Martha Nichols, trans. (Berkeley: University of California Press, 1995), 353.

8. Rosemary O'Neill, *Art and Visual Culture on the French Riviera, 1956–1971* (Oxfordshire: Routledge, 2016), 124, n. 80.

9. *Mirrors and Portraits*, exh. cat. (Los Angeles: Dwan Gallery, 1963).

10. Restany, *Martial Raysse,* exh. cat., trans. Neil A. Levine (New York: Alexander Iolas Gallery, Nov. 24–Dec 1964), n.p.

11. Raysse, *Martial Raysse, Maître et esclave de l'imagination,* exh. cat. (Amsterdam: Stedelijk Museum, 1965), n.p. Trans. Gherghescu, "Timeline," in *Martial Raysse*, 470.

12. Otto Hahn, "Martial Raysse ou l'obsession solaire," *Journal des arts plastiques* no. 31 (February 1967). Trans. Gherghescu, "Timeline," in *Martial Raysse*, 475.

13. Raysse, "J'ai mille choses à classer...", *Collage* no. 6 (September 1969): 69. Trans. Gherghescu, "Timeline," in *Martial Raysse*, 472.

14. Raysse, "Lettre à Marzotto," Paris, March 9, 1968. Trans. Gherghescu, "Timeline," in *Martial Raysse*, 475.

15. Raysse, excerpt from poster-manifesto drawn up for the exhibition *Une forme en liberté,* Galerie Alexander Iolas, Paris, September–October 1969. Trans. Gherghescu, "Timeline," in *Martial Raysse*, 476.

16. Raysse, quoted by Jean Clay, "Pourquoi les artistes tournent le dos à l'art," *Réalités* no. 316 (May 1972): 100. Trans. Gherghescu, "Timeline," in *Martial Raysse*, 476.

17. Trans. Gherghescu, "Timeline," in *Martial Raysse*, 482.

18. Raysse, in *Martial Raysse*, exh. cat., Dominique Stella, ed. Trans. Gherghescu, "Timeline," in *Martial Raysse*, 484.

19. Pontus Hultén, in *Martial Raysse 1970–1980,* exh. cat. (Paris: Centre Pompidou, 1981), 3. Trans. Gherghescu, "Timeline," in *Martial Raysse*, 483.

20. Trans. Gherghescu, "Timeline," in *Martial Raysse*, 484.

Checklist of the Exhibition

Page 31
PORTRAIT DE GABRIELLA LA JOLIE VÉNITIENNE
1963
Mixed media on canvas
34 ⅝ × 24 7⁄16 × 3 ¾ inches (88 × 62 × 9.5 cm)
Private collection

Page 35
T'ENVOLERAS TU . . . SANS REGRETS
2015
Acrylic on canvas
11 13⁄16 × 11 13⁄16 inches (30 × 30 cm)
Private collection

Pages 37; 38–39, 119 (details); cover
IMPASSE DES SOUPIRS
2010
Acrylic on canvas mounted to wood
32 ¼ × 26 1⁄16 inches (82 × 66.2 cm)
Private collection

Pages 41; 1, 42–43 (details)
QUE VEUX TU DIRE MON BEL AMI
2017
Acrylic on canvas
44 ½ × 35 7⁄16 inches (113 × 90 cm)
Private collection

Page 45
AH ! D'ACCORD L'EXTRÊME
2016
Acrylic on canvas
60 × 52 inches (152.5 × 132 cm)
Private collection

Page 47
QUOI ! VAN RIJN NON NON VAN DEN EECKHOUT
2017
Acrylic on canvas mounted to wood
35 × 24 13⁄16 inches (89 × 63 cm)
Private collection

Pages 49; 118 (detail)
LE JOUR OÙ GILBERT S'EST NOYÉ
2012
Acrylic on canvas
56 5⁄16 × 35 7⁄16 inches (143 × 90 cm)
Private collection

Page 50
BEL AMOUR
1998
Distemper on canvas board
10 ⅝ × 12 ⅝ inches (27 × 32 cm)
Private collection

Pages 51; 52–53 (detail)
CES DEUX GARS-LÀ
2008
Acrylic on canvas
47 ¼ × 47 ¼ inches (120 × 120 cm)
Private collection

Page 55
LE FUN SOLANGE !
2014
Oil on canvas
31 ⅞ × 25 9⁄16 inches (81 x 65 cm)
Private collection, New York

Pages 57; 58–59 (detail)
MAIS OUI PULCHRA !
2016
Acrylic on canvas
63 ⅜ × 43 11⁄16 inches (161 × 111 cm)
Private collection

Pages 61; 120 (detail)
COMME C'EST TRISTE LA TRISTESSE
2011
Acrylic on canvas
26 × 23 ¼ inches (66 × 59 cm)
Private collection

Pages 63; 2 (detail)
SONGEUSE ROXANE
2013
Distemper on canvas
24 13/16 × 24 13/16 inches (63 × 63 cm)
Private collection

Page 64
LA LAGUNE LAURA
2016
Acrylic on canvas
11 13/16 × 11 13/16 inches (30 × 30 cm)
Private collection

Pages 65; 117 (detail)
ANTONINA LEI VA BALLARE QUESTA SERA
2017
Oil on canvas
19 11/16 × 19 11/16 inches (50 × 50 cm)
Private collection

Pages 67; 68–69, 116 (details)
NOW
2017
Acrylic on canvas
82 1/4 × 69 1/16 inches (209 × 175.5 cm)
Private collection

Pages 71; 4, 72–73 (details)
UN BEAU MERLE
2008
Acrylic on paper mounted to board
31 1/2 × 23 1/4 inches (80 × 59 cm)
Private collection

Page 75
Ô LÉA !
2013
Acrylic on canvas
15 3/4 × 15 3/4 inches (40 × 40 cm)
Private collection

Pages 77; 3, 78–79 (details)
THAT ONE OUT OF GREEN DREAM
2017
Acrylic on canvas
11 13/16 × 11 13/16 inches (30 × 30 cm)
Private collection

Page 81
DIRIEZ VOUS : POÉSIE ?
2014
Acrylic on canvas
25 9/16 × 19 11/16 inches (65 × 50 cm)
Private collection

Pages 82; 5 (detail)
SI SEUL....
2016
Acrylic on canvas
15 3/4 × 15 3/4 inches (40 × 40 cm)
Private collection

Page 83
IL VAUT MIEUX NE PAS Y PENSER LAURENT
2017
Acrylic on canvas
23 5/8 × 23 5/8 inches (60 × 60 cm)
Private collection

Pages 85; 86–87 (detail)
FERVEUR OBSCURE
2012
Acrylic on canvas
28 3/4 × 23 5/8 inches (73 × 60 cm)
Private collection

PHOTOGRAPH CREDITS

Pages 8, 28, 92–93, 113: Jean-Francois Jaussaud

Front cover, 1, 2, 3, 4, 5, 31, 35, 37, 38–39, 41, 42–43, 45, 47, 49, 50, 51, 52–53, 57, 58–59, 61, 63, 64, 65, 67, 68–69, 71, 72–73, 75, 77, 78–79, 81, 82, 83, 85, 86–87, 106, 116, 117, 118, 119, 120: Elisabeth Bernstein

Page 55: Stefan Altenburger

Pages 12, 23, 88, 94: Photograph © Christer Strömholm

Page 14: Photograph Cathy Carver, courtesy Hirshhorn Museum and Sculpture Garden, Smithsonian Institution

Pages 15, 17 (top and bottom), 19 (left and right), 21: Courtesy Inventaire Martial Raysse

Page 18: Photograph Matteo De Fina © Palazzo Grassi

Pages 95, 96 (right): Photograph Shunk-Kender © J. Paul Getty Trust. Getty Research Institute, Los Angeles (2014.R.20); work by Arman © 2018 Artists Rights Society (ARS), New York / ADAGP, Paris

Page 96 (left): Photograph © 2018 Yves Klein Estate, Artists Rights Society (ARS), New York / ADAGP, Paris

Page 97 (left): Courtesy Luxembourg + Dayan

Page 97 (right): Photograph Ed van der Elsken, courtesy Nederlands Fotomuseum

Page 98: Dwan Gallery (Los Angeles, California, and New York, New York) records, 1959–circa 1982, bulk 1959–1971. Archives of American Art, Smithsonian Institution

Page 99: Photograph Active Museum / Alamy Stock Photo

Page 100: Photograph Eric Sutherland for Walker Art Center

Page 101 (left): Photograph Hervé Véronèse, Musée National d'Art Moderne, Centre Georges Pompidou © CNAC/MNAM/Dist. RMN-Grand Palais / Art Resource, NY

Page 101 (right): Photograph Erio Piccagliani © Teatro alla Scala

Page 102: Photograph © De Fina Matteo / Palazzo Grassi, Venise

Page 104: Photograph 12 / Alamy Stock Photo

Page 105: Photograph Hemis / Alamy Stock Photo

Page 107: Photograph LAGOS CID Manuel/Paris Match Collection/Getty Images

Page 108: Photograph Patrick Kovarik/AFP/Getty Images

Page 109: Photograph Fulvio Orsenigo, © Palazzo Grassi, ORCH orsenigo_chemollo

Unless otherwise stated, the photographs in this catalogue were made available by the institutions of private lenders named as their owners or by the artist. We have made every effort to locate all copyright holders. Any errors or omissions will be corrected in subsequent editions.

TEXT CREDITS

"Martial Raysse: Je suis un poète" © Jane Livingston

"Promenade avec vue sur Bacchus, le pain et le vin" © Martial Raysse

"Promenade with thoughts on Bacchus, bread, and wine" © Martial Raysse. Translation © Charles Penwarden, 2018

Quote by Martial Raysse (page 30), quoted in Olivier Céna, "La toile à zero," *Télérama*, December 16, 1992

Excerpt from "Qu'il est long le chemin" © Martial Raysse. Published by Editions Galerie kamel mennour, Paris, 2012

Excerpt from "How the path is long" © Martial Raysse; published by Editions Galerie kamel mennour, Paris, 2012

"The Bird" © Leopoldine Core

"I have a thousand things to put in order" © Martial Raysse; originally published in *Martial Raysse*, Dwan Gallery, Los Angeles, 1967

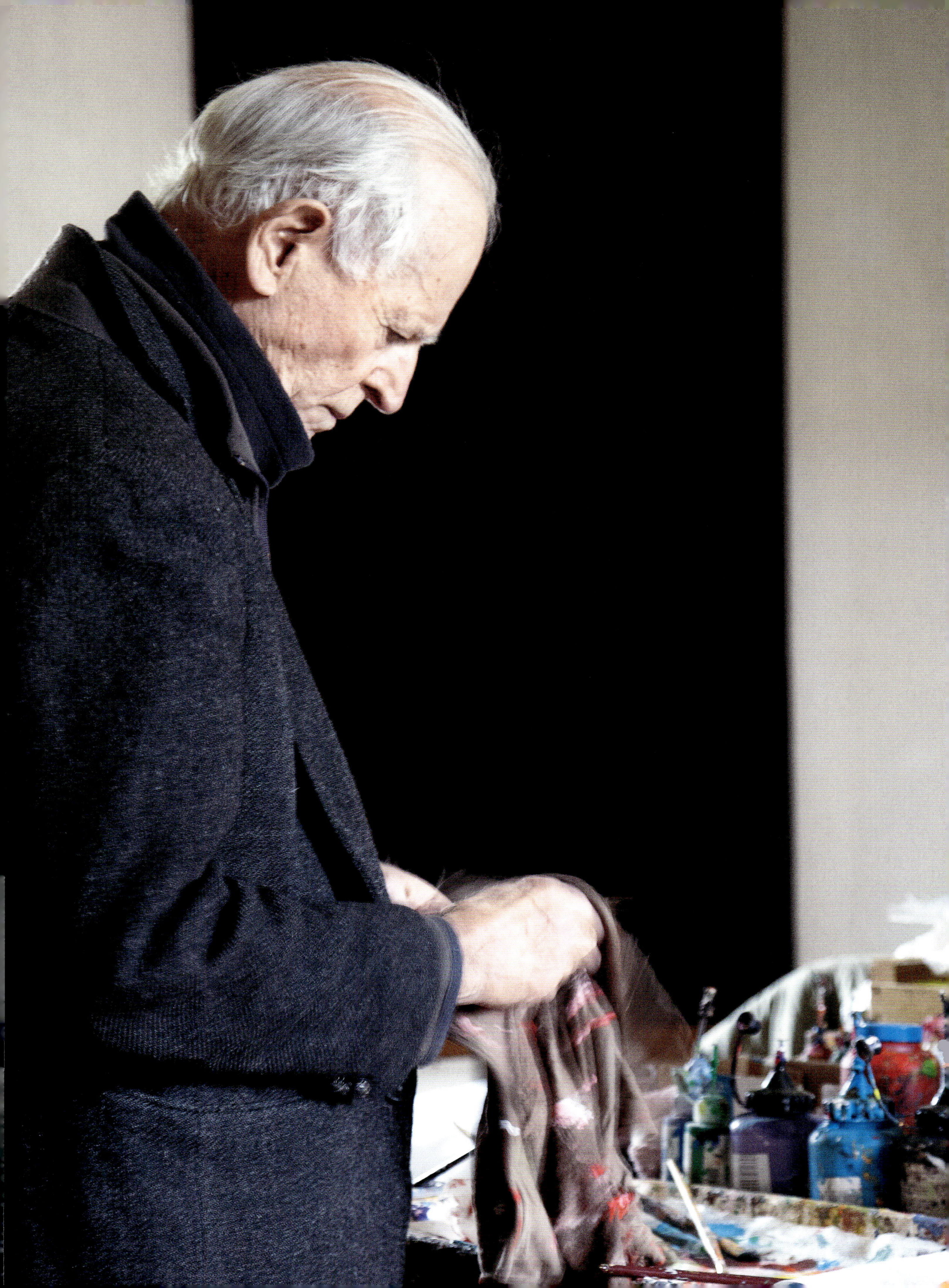

Published on the occasion of the exhibition

MARTIAL RAYSSE: VISAGES
February 28–April 14, 2018

ĹG
LÉVY GORVY

909 Madison Avenue
New York, NY 10021
+1 212 772 2004
levygorvy.com

Founders: Dominique Lévy and Brett Gorvy
Director of Operations: Cari Brentegani
Director of Exhibitions & Publications: Clara Touboul
Exhibitions & Publications Coordinator: Amelia Brown
Exhibition Researcher: Courtney Fiske
Registrar: Jess Pillar

Design: McCall Associates, New York
Printing and Binding: Trifolio SRL, Verona
Editing: Susan Delson

ISBN: 978-1-944379-23-0

Printed in bound in Verona and available through
ARTBOOK | D.A.P.
75 Broad Street, Suite 630, New York, NY 10004
Tel: (212) 627-1999 Fax: (212) 627-9484

Cover: *Impasse des soupirs* (see page 37)
Pages 8, 28, 92–93, 113: Martial Raysse at his studio in Bergerac, 2017. Photograph Jean-Francois Jaussaud

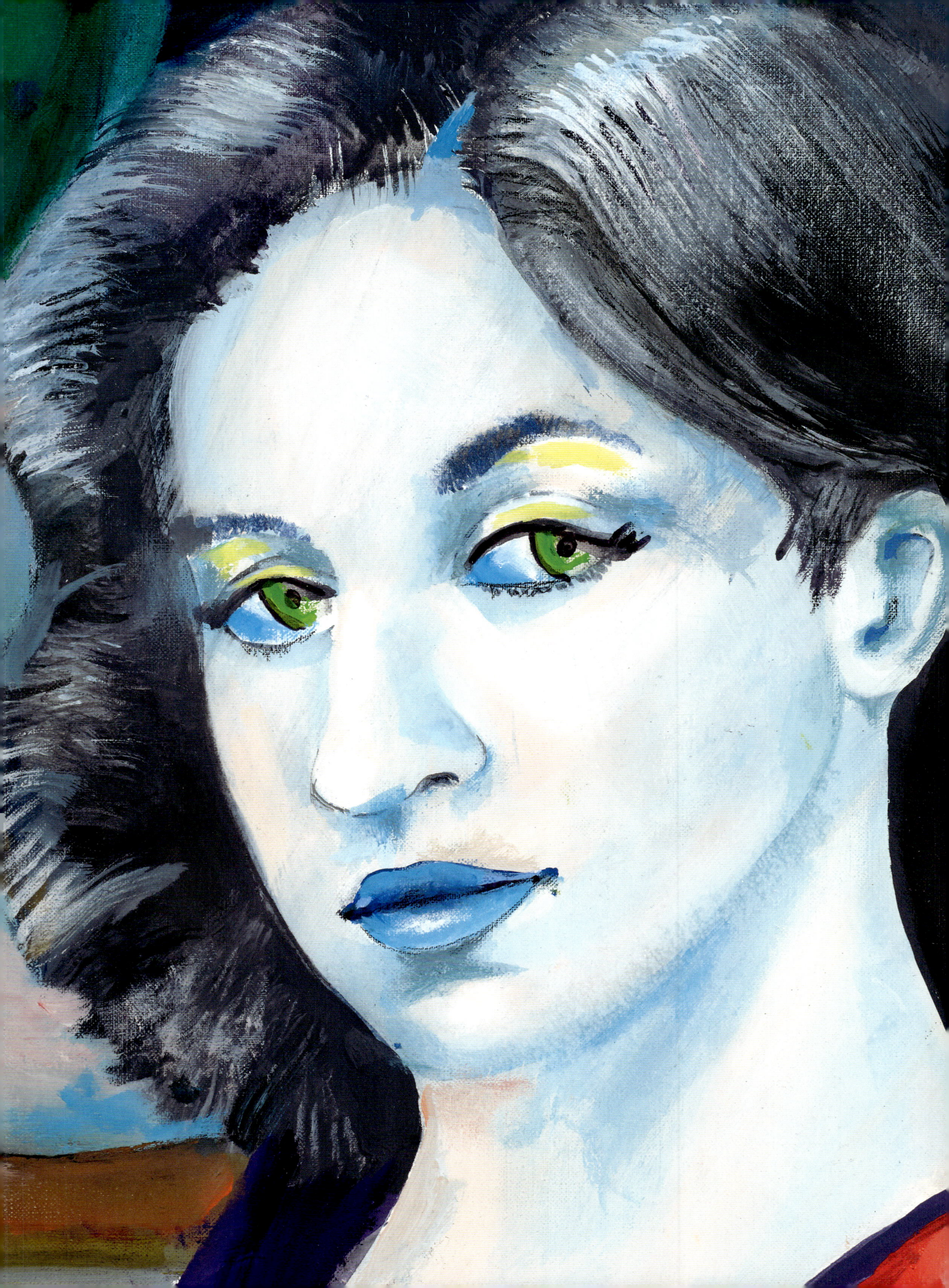

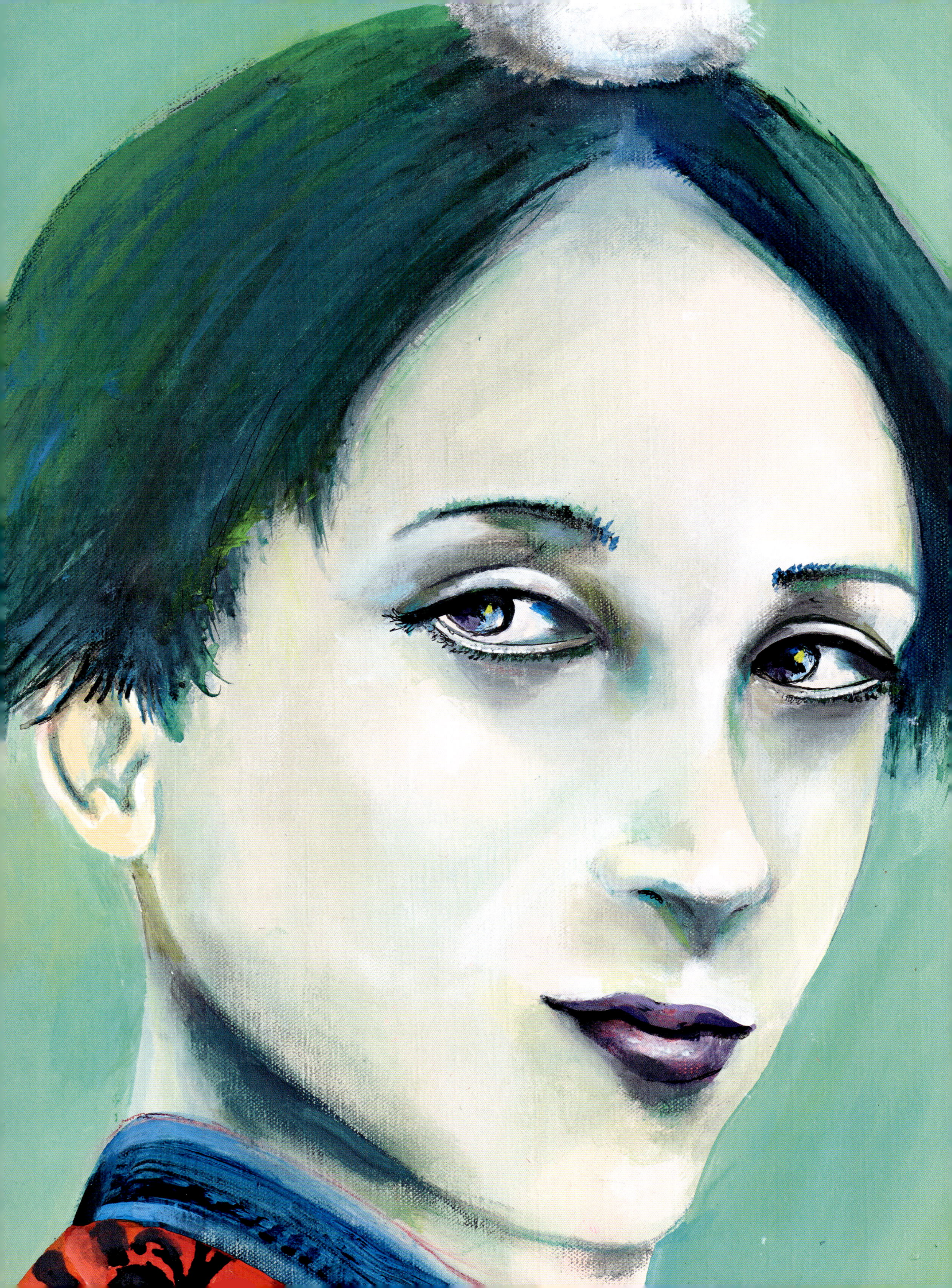

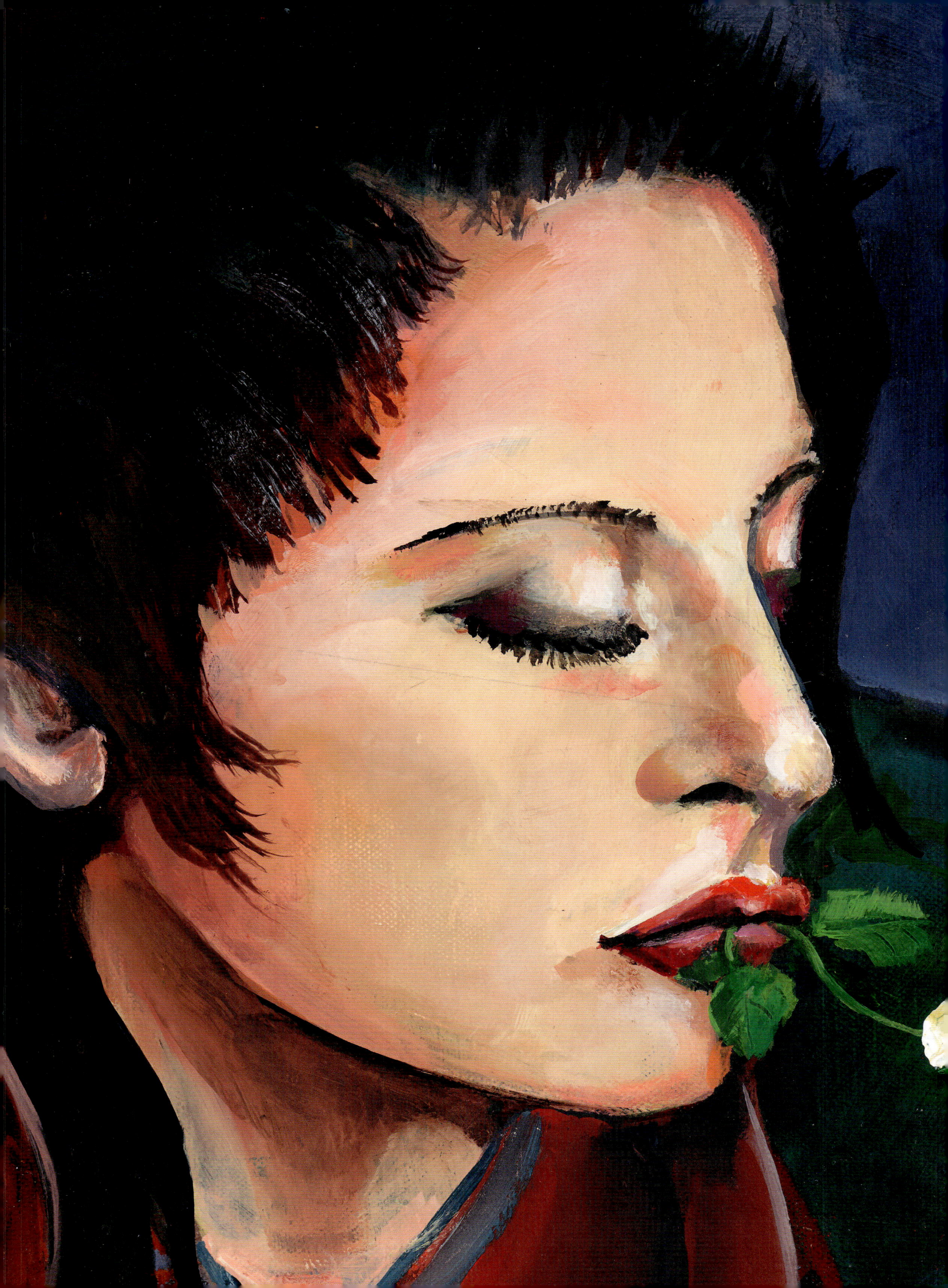

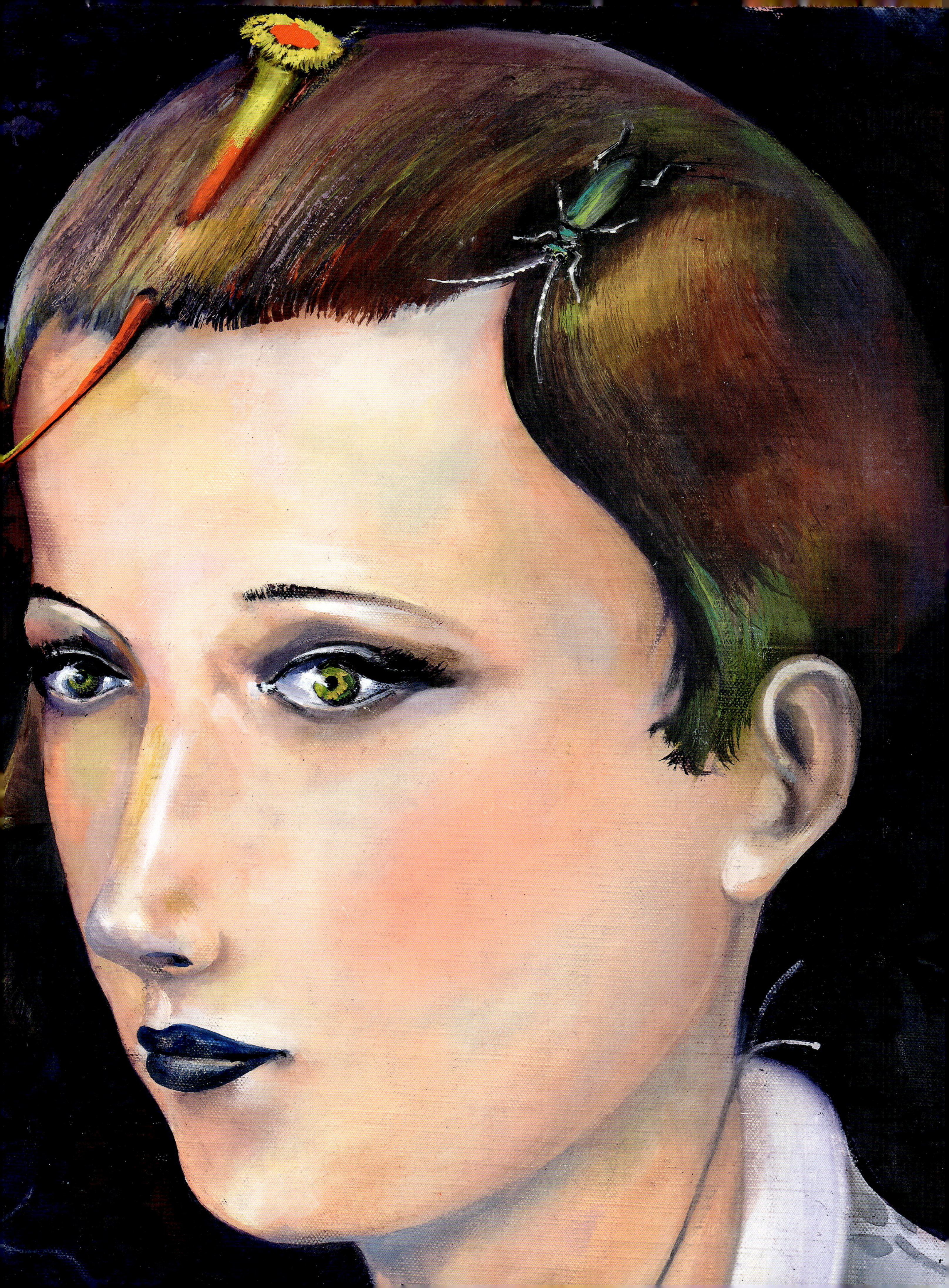

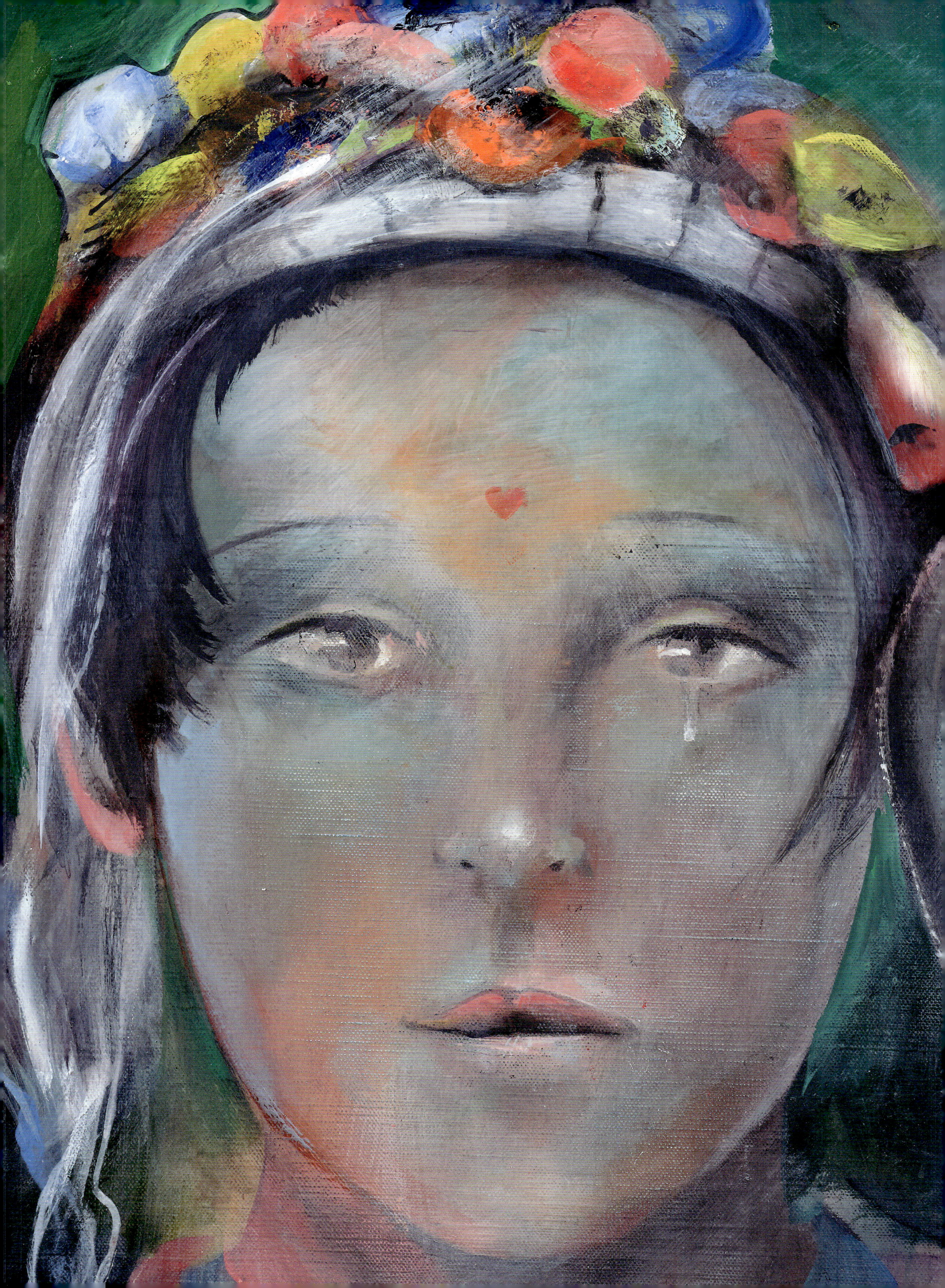